Foreword

All of us remember stories from the Bible. They are part of the fabric of our lives, woven from our childhood and made strong in our adult world. David and Goliath, Daniel in the lions' den, Noah and his ark—they are a part of our Catholic faith, our earliest memories in religious education.

Contained in this book are these well-known stories of faith and heroism. It is our role as Christian parents to introduce the timeless message of these stories to a new generation. Too many of us feel uncomfortable teaching our children about the faith. It is a task we would rather pass on to the professional educator, the Sunday-school volunteer, or the parish priest.

But our children learn from us first and foremost, especially in matters of faith. It happens whether we wish that to be true or not. Bible stories present the easiest introduction to family religious education. With stories that entertain and enthrall, we can begin the process of introducing our children to God and His eternal love for us.

Take the time to read these stories to your children. As your children grow, let them read it. This is a book meant to be used—to be dropped and scuffed and spilled upon. Let's not allow it to gather dust. A whole new world of faith is about to open up between you and your children.

Robert P. Lockwood, publisher, *Our Sunday Visitor*

For centuries, in their own search for purpose and goodness in life, men and women have found extraordinary examples in the people whose lives the Scriptures record. Despite the differences that passing time or geography may create, the faith of Abraham, the courage of Esther, and the struggle of Job have lessons for everyone. Surely that is true of the great model that we possess in the undaunted faith and virtue of Mary, and certainly in the sublime example that we have in the life, and death, of the Lord Jesus.

These Bible stories for children serve a great purpose. In language and form appropriate for young readers, these stories give strong lessons in values. Acquainting young minds now with the Bible not only informs them of our examples in faith that are the men and women of the Scriptures but directs them to the Scriptures themselves for future reading and instruction.

These stories are not the Bible itself. They reflect, and lead to, the Bible. Parents well may serve their children best by reading the stories to their children, explaining their meaning, and above all, by repeating the faith and dedication displayed by the figures in the stories in their own lives.

We pray for parents who seek to give their children the greatest of life's gifts, an awareness of God, trust in Him, and love for Him. Most especially, we pray for the young who will hear, or read, these stories. The Lord Himself asked that they be brought to Him. Through these stories, and indeed through the Holy Bible itself, may our young readers see beyond human experience the vision of God in earthly life, and finally the Beatific Vision itself in heaven.

Reverend Owen F. Campion, associate publisher,
Our Sunday Visitor

This Catholic Family-Time Bible Stories
in Pictures *belongs to*

_____

Presented on

_____

By

_____

_____

· *Catholic* ·
Family-Time
BIBLE
STORIES
IN PICTURES

Kenneth N. Taylor

Editorial Assistant, Carole Newing Johnson

OUR SUNDAY VISITOR
Huntington, Indiana

Illustrations: Pages 57, 157, 159, 164-165, 299 copyright © 1989 by Robert Florczack; Front cover (sun stands still), pages 92-93, 94-97, 99, 100-101, 102-103, 104-105, 149, 151, 153, 155, 167, 169, 181 copyright © 1989 by Don Gabriel; Front cover (ark and rainbow), pages 11, 12-13, 14-15, 17, 19, 107, 109, 110-111, 117, 119, 121, 124-125, 127, 128-129, 131, 133, 135, 136-137, 138-139, 140-141, 170 copyright © 1989 by Blas Gallego; Pages 22-23, 84-85, 144-145, 182-183, 236-237, 272-273 copyright © 1989 by Al Lorenz; Pages 33, 35, 36, 41, 43, 115, 161, 195, 241, 243 copyright © 1989 by Sergio Martinez; Front cover (Saul escapes), pages 21, 25, 26-27, 30-31, 58-59, 61, 64-65, 66-67, 69, 70-71, 74, 76-77, 78-79, 82-83, 87, 289, 291, 293, 295, 297 copyright © by Joseph Miralles; Cover spine (Adam and Eve), pages 7, 9, 45, 47, 49, 51, 53, 91, 113, 143, 147, 173, 175, 177, 179 copyright © 1989 by Joan Pelaez.

All other illustrations copyright © 1989 by Tyndale House Publishers, Inc. All rights reserved. Page 303 by Ron DiCianni; Cover (Jesus / disciples), pages 163, 185, 187, 188-189, 193, 197, 199, 201, 203, 204-205, 207, 209, 211, 213, 215, 217, 218-219, 221, 223, 224-225, 226-227, 230-231, 233, 235, 239, 245, 247, 249, 250-251, 253, 255, 258-259, 261, 263, 265, 267, 269, 270, 275, 277, 278-279, 281-282, 284, 287 by Donald Kueker; Pages 3, 4, 5, 81, 88-89 by Jeffrey Terreson.

Library of Congress Cataloging-in-Publication Data

Taylor, Kenneth Nathaniel.
   The Catholic family-time Bible stories in pictures / Kenneth N. Taylor; editorial assistant, Carole Newing Johnson.
     p.   cm.
   Summary: Includes over one hundred brief Bible stories from both the Old and New Testaments, with illustrations and some discussion questions.
   ISBN 0-87973-882-0
   1. Bible stories, English. [1. Bible stories.] I. Title.
BS551.2.T374   1992
220.9'505—dc20
                                           92-22166

Contents

A Word to Parents

Young children are wide open to spiritual truth—more than children will be at any later age. Now is the best time to read Bible stories to them, and soon, to read to them directly from the Bible. Here in this book are stories that every child should know.

Regular after-supper family times that include Bible reading and prayer are of great value. This book can be a first step in establishing this fruitful habit.

Pray regularly for your children, and bring them up in the joy and fear of the Lord. May God answer all your prayers and give your children the strong support they will need during all their coming years. May it be true of them that "from childhood they have known the Holy Scriptures that are able to make them wise unto salvation through faith in Christ Jesus."

Kenneth N. Taylor

God Makes a Beautiful World

Long ago, God made the world out of nothing. But it didn't look the way it does now. There were no people, animals, birds, trees, or flowers. Everything was lonely and dark. So God made the light. He gave the light the name *Day.* He called the darkness *Night.* This was the first day of creation.

On the second day of creation, God made the sky. He named the sky *Heaven.* And on the third day, God made the oceans and lakes and the dry land. Then he made the grass grow and covered the land with all kinds of flowers, bushes, and trees.

The fourth day God put the sun, moon, and stars in the sky.

On the fifth day, God made all the wonderful fish in the sea, big and small. He made all the

birds, too—ducks and geese that could swim, eagles and robins to live in the woods and fields.

Then, on the sixth day, he made the animals—rabbits, elephants, and even bees—he made them all! And God was very pleased with what he had made. It was all beautiful and good! The seventh day, God rested. It was a quiet and different day from all the other days, a holy day of rest.

Let's thank God
now
for the
beautiful
world he
has made.
Can you think of some
ways you can help keep
it beautiful? GENESIS 1

God Makes Adam and Eve

On the day God made all the animals, he made the first man and named him Adam. God shaped him out of dust from the ground and breathed into him to make him alive.

God put Adam in a beautiful garden to live. But Adam was lonely because he was the only person in all the world. So God put him to sleep and took one of his ribs and made a woman from it. Her name was Eve, and she became Adam's wife. So Adam and Eve lived together in the Garden of Eden. They were very happy, and they were special friends of God.

God told Adam and Eve to take care of the garden. He also told them to eat any food in the garden except the fruit from the Tree of the Knowledge of Good and Evil.

You are an amazing creation. Look at the way your hand moves! Listen to the noises around you. You can hear! Let's thank God now for making you so wonderful. GENESIS 2

The World's Saddest Day

There was a wicked spirit named Satan in the garden with Adam and Eve. He was disguised as a beautiful snake. He came to Eve and told her to eat the fruit God said not to eat. "God is bad," Satan told her. "That fruit is good for you." Satan was lying, but Eve believed him instead of believing God. She looked at the forbidden tree. Its fruit looked so good that she took some and ate it. Then she gave some of it to Adam, and he ate it too. What a sad day! Adam and Eve disobeyed God. Now there was sin in the world. And God punished them and sent them out of the beautiful garden!

What did Satan tell Eve? What did Eve do? How did God punish Adam and Eve for disobeying him?
GENESIS 3

8

Cain Kills Abel

Adam and Eve had a son named Cain. He was a farmer and grew lots of fruits and vegetables. His brother, Abel, was a shepherd and had a flock of sheep. Both Cain and Abel had sinful hearts, like their parents. But Abel was sorry about his sins. He brought a lamb from his flock as an offering to God so that God would forgive him. God wanted Cain to sacrifice a lamb, too. But Cain didn't do what God wanted. He gave God vegetables from his farm instead. God was pleased with Abel's gift, but not with Cain's. This made Cain very angry. He wanted to get even. So one day when they were alone, Cain killed Abel! How sad this made God! God told Cain that he would never have a home to call his own. This was his punishment for killing Abel.

Do you ever get angry? Let's ask God now to help you when you are angry. Ask God to help you get rid of your anger before it makes you do something wrong.
GENESIS 4

Noah Builds an Ark

Many years went by. The world became more and more wicked. People did all kinds of bad things. This made God angry because he hates sin. God said he would punish the people. He would send

water to cover the earth so everyone would drown. But there was one good man, whose name was Noah. God told Noah to build a huge boat to save himself and his family from the flood. Noah believed God. He built a giant ark with a big door in the side. Noah also warned all the people. He told them God would send a flood because of their sins. But the people just laughed at Noah. They were not sorry for their sins.

Why was God going to send a flood? What did God tell Noah to do? What did all the other people do?

GENESIS 6

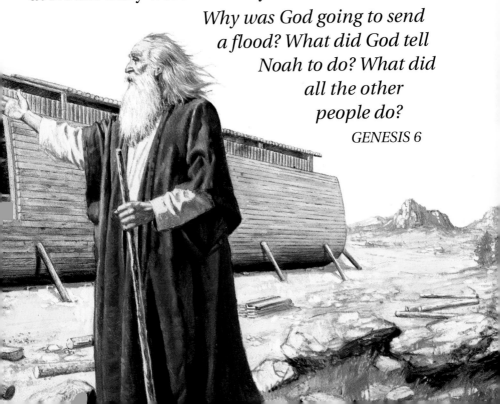

Saved from Drowning

God told Noah to fill the ark with birds and animals. So Noah brought a father and mother animal of every kind into the ark. Then he and his family went inside, and God closed the door behind them and locked it so no one else could get in.

Then the rains came. It rained and rained and rained for forty days and forty nights. Soon the ground was covered with water, and the ark floated away. Even the hills and mountains were

covered with water. So all the people, animals, and birds were drowned except those inside the ark.

After a long time, the water began to go away. The ark came to rest on top of a mountain called Ararat. God finally told Noah it was time to come out of the ark. Then Noah built an altar and sacrificed animals and birds upon it to thank God for saving his family from drowning in the Flood. God promised never to send another flood to drown all the people. As a reminder of his promise, God put a big rainbow in the sky. Noah could see this rainbow when it rained, and he remembered God's promise.

A rainbow reminds us that God always keeps his promises. Can you think of another promise God has made? Can you think of a promise you made but then didn't keep? GENESIS 7–9

The Tower of Babel

After the Flood, Noah and his family had many children and grandchildren. Soon there were thousands and thousands of people in the world again. These people did all sorts of bad things just like the people who lived before the Flood.

One day the people decided to build a huge tower as high as heaven. They wanted to show how great they were. They were very proud. But it is sinful to be proud, and God knew what they were thinking. So God decided to stop the people from building the tower. He made them speak in different languages.

If one man asked another for a hammer, the other man didn't know what he was saying. This made them angry with each other.

The people couldn't work with each other any-more because they couldn't understand each other's words. So they all left the tower, and those speaking the same languages formed groups and moved away. That is why different languages are spoken in different parts of the world today. The tower was called the Tower of Babel because it was there that God mixed up their languages.

Why did the people want to build the tower? What did God do?
GENESIS 11

God's Friend Abraham

Far away in a land called Ur (we call it Iraq today) there lived a man named Abram. One day God told Abram to move to another country. Abram obeyed God. He took his family and all his sheep and goats and cows and made the long journey to the land that God showed him. This land was called Canaan. Today we call it Israel. And God told Abram, "I will give all this land to you. It will belong to you and to your children forever." And God blessed Abram and took care of him.

One day God told Abram, "I am your friend." Then Abram reminded God that he wanted a son. Abram had no children, and he was getting very old. God took Abram out under the night sky and showed him the millions of stars. Then God told him, "You will not only have a son, but many, many grandchildren and great-

grandchil-
dren too.
Their families
will be like
those stars
up there—too
many to count.
And they will become
a great nation!" And
God gave Abram
a new name—
Abraham. *Abraham* means "the father of a great
nation."

*Abraham obeyed God, and God took care of
him. God was his friend. God wants to be your
friend, too, and he wants you to obey him just like
Abraham did.* GENESIS 12; 15

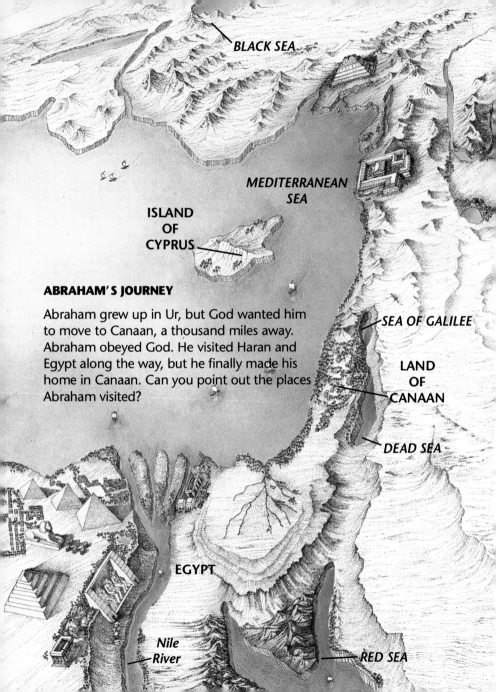

BLACK SEA

MEDITERRANEAN
SEA

ISLAND
OF
CYPRUS

ABRAHAM'S JOURNEY

Abraham grew up in Ur, but God wanted him
to move to Canaan, a thousand miles away.
Abraham obeyed God. He visited Haran and
Egypt along the way, but he finally made his
home in Canaan. Can you point out the places
Abraham visited?

SEA OF GALILEE

LAND
OF
CANAAN

DEAD SEA

EGYPT

Nile
River

RED SEA

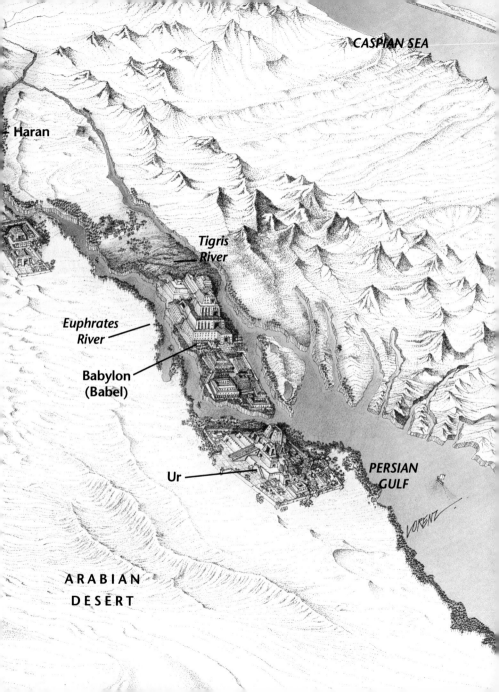

CASPIAN SEA

Haran

Tigris
River

Euphrates
River

Babylon
(Babel)

Ur

PERSIAN
GULF

LORENZ

ARABIAN
DESERT

Abraham Shares with Lot

Abraham's nephew Lot traveled with him to the land God promised to give to Abraham. Abraham and Lot both became very rich. Each of them owned many cows, goats, and sheep. Soon there were so many animals that there wasn't enough grass for them to eat. Then the men who took care of Lot's animals began to argue and fight with the men who took care of Abraham's animals.

"Let's not have any fighting among us," Abraham said to Lot. So they divided the land between them. Abraham let Lot have the best land. It had the most grass for Lot's animals to eat. But Abraham didn't care. He knew God would take care of him.

Then God told Abraham, "Someday, the good land Lot chose will all be yours!"

It's better to be a giver than a taker. What is one way you can share and be like Abraham?
GENESIS 13

God Rescues Lot

One day three men came to visit Abraham. Now these three men were really not men at all. Two of them were angels, and the other one was God. God told Abraham that he had decided to destroy the cities of Sodom and Gomorrah because the people there were so bad. Abraham was very sad when he heard this because his nephew Lot lived in Sodom.

"Perhaps there are some good people living in the city," he said to God. "Must they die too?"

God listened to Abraham and said, "If there are only ten good people there, I will not destroy the city."

The two angels went to Sodom. But there were

not even ten good people there. So the angels warned Lot that God was going to destroy the city. Lot was very sad to leave his home. The angels had to drag him and his wife and two daughters out of the city to save them.

"Run to the mountains where the fire won't kill you," the angels told them. "And don't look back."

Then God sent down fire from heaven and destroyed Sodom and Gomorrah. But Lot's wife disobeyed the angels and looked back. So she died right there and became a statue of salt.

Why did Lot's wife turn into a statue of salt?
GENESIS 18–19

Abraham Gives Isaac to God

God had promised to give Abraham and Sarah a son. But years and years went by, and Sarah didn't have a baby. Then finally, when Abraham was 100 years old, a baby boy was born to them. They named him Isaac. What a happy day it was when God's promise finally came true!

One day, when Isaac was a teenager, God told Abraham to go to Mount Moriah and sacrifice Isaac on an altar. What? How could Abraham kill his own dear son? But Abraham knew that he must do what-

ever God said. He knew that God could bring Isaac back to life again. So Abraham and Isaac

traveled to Mount Moriah. Abraham laid Isaac
on the altar. Then he raised his knife to sacrifice
the son he loved so much.

Suddenly, the angel of God shouted from
heaven, "Abraham! Stop!" The angel told Abraham not to hurt Isaac. He said that Abraham had
proved that he loved God and would do whatever

God told him to. Then Abraham saw a ram caught in the bushes by its horns. God had sent it there to use as a sacrifice instead of Isaac. Abraham killed the ram and burned it on the altar. God was very pleased with Abraham for being willing to obey.

What did God tell Abraham to do? Was Abraham willing to obey God? GENESIS 22–24

God Answers a Prayer

Abraham sent his most trustworthy servant to find Isaac a wife who loved God. How could this servant pick the right wife for Isaac? He asked God to help him. And God did! The servant decided to wait by the town well. When a girl came to the well for water, he would ask her for a drink. If she was kind and also offered to water his thirsty camels, he would know she was the right one. And that is just what happened when Rebekah came to the well! She drew water for him to drink and for his camels, too. Then the servant thanked God for answering his prayer.

Have you asked God to help you with something this week? What are some of the ways he might answer your prayer? GENESIS 24

Esau's Terrible Mistake

Isaac and Rebekah had two sons. Their names were Esau and Jacob. In those days, the oldest son in every family had what was called a *birthright*. This means he got most of the money and property when his father died. Esau was the oldest son, so the birthright belonged to him. But Jacob wanted it. One day Esau came home from a hunting trip. He was tired and hungry. Jacob had made some especially good food, and Esau asked for some. Jacob said Esau could have it if he would give Jacob his birthright! Esau didn't care about his birthright right then because he was so hungry, so he said Jacob could have it. Then Jacob gave him some food.

It was wrong for Esau to trade his birthright for some food. God wanted him to keep the birthright, but he sold it instead.

*What was a birthright? How much did Jacob
pay Esau for it?* GENESIS 25

Jacob Lies to His Father

Isaac was getting very old and couldn't see. One day he asked Esau, his oldest son, to go out and catch a deer. Isaac told him, "Cook the meat just the way I like it best. After that I will bless you." He meant that he would ask God to be kind to Esau and give him many good things. So Esau went out to hunt.

But Isaac's wife, Rebecca, didn't want Esau to get the blessing. She wanted the best for Esau's brother, Jacob. So Rebecca cooked some lamb meat so that it tasted just like the deer meat Isaac loved. Then she got Jacob some of Esau's clothes to put on. She also put some goatskins on his neck and hands so that he felt just like hairy Esau.

Jacob took the food to his father. Because Isaac was old and almost blind, he couldn't see who

Jacob was. Isaac asked if he really was Esau, and Jacob said yes. Isaac felt Jacob's hairy neck and smelled his clothes. Isaac thought Jacob was Esau. So Isaac ate the food and blessed him.

This was a very bad thing that Jacob and his mother did. Jacob should not have lied to his father. And when Esau came home and discovered the trick, he was very angry. He was so angry that he said he would kill Jacob someday.

How did Rebekah and Jacob trick Isaac?
GENESIS 27

Jacob Leaves Home

Rebecca and Isaac sent Jacob to a far-off land where his uncle Laban lived. They wanted him to find a girl to marry who loved God. One night, while he was traveling, Jacob had a dream. He saw some stairs in

front of him reaching to heaven. Angels were going up and down them, and God stood at the top of the stairs. God told Jacob about the country that he was going to give to him and his children. He told Jacob that he would be with him and take care of him wherever he went. When Jacob woke up, he called the place Bethel. *Bethel* means "the house of God."

At his uncle Laban's house, Jacob met

Laban's daughter Rachel. He grew to love Rachel very much. So Jacob told his uncle that he would work for him seven years if he could marry Rachel afterwards. This made Laban very happy.

Jacob worked for seven years. But when the time was up, Laban said Jacob had to marry Leah, Rachel's older sister, first. Jacob had to work seven more years for Rachel! This was very unfair of Laban. But Jacob agreed to it because of his love for Rachel.

And God blessed Jacob. He grew very rich and had many camels, donkeys, and flocks of sheep and goats.

How long did Jacob have to work for Laban? Why did Jacob have to work so long? GENESIS 28–31

Is Esau Still Angry?

After Jacob had lived with his uncle Laban for a long time, he decided to move back to the land where his father and mother lived. So Jacob put his wives and children on camels, took all of his goats and other animals, and started the long, long walk. They walked for many weeks.

But Jacob was afraid. Soon he would meet his brother, Esau, again. Esau might try to kill him for stealing his birthright many years before. Jacob sent servants on ahead with camels, cows, goats, sheep, and donkeys as gifts for Esau. Then Jacob saw Esau marching toward him with four hundred men! But Esau did not attack Jacob. Instead, he ran to Jacob and hugged him.

God had promised Jacob at Bethel that he would be with him and keep him from harm.

One way God kept this promise was to take away Esau's anger and help him forgive Jacob.

When someone hurts you, do you try to get even or do you forgive like Esau forgave Jacob? Can you think of someone you should forgive? GENESIS 32–33

Joseph's Strange Dreams

Joseph was one of Jacob's twelve sons. He was the youngest except for Benjamin. Joseph was his father's favorite son, so his father gave him a present of a beautiful coat. But this made his brothers very jealous.

One night Joseph had a strange dream. In the dream, he and his brothers were tying bundles of grain in the fields. Then his brothers' bundles bowed down to his bundle. When Joseph told his brothers about his dream, they got very angry at him. They thought Joseph was saying that he was better then they were! Another night Joseph dreamed that the sun, moon, and eleven stars all bowed down to him. This meant that his father and mother, as well as his brothers, would bow to him. Even his father said he was foolish to think this would happen. But God had a special plan for Joseph.

Why were Joseph's brothers jealous? What did Joseph dream? GENESIS 37

Joseph Is Sold

One day Joseph went out into the fields to take his brothers some food. They saw him coming and said, "Here comes that dreamer. Let's kill him and throw him into a well."

But Joseph's brother Reuben got them to put Joseph into an empty well alive. Reuben planned to come back and pull Joseph out. But when Reuben wasn't around, his brothers pulled Joseph out of the well and sold him to some men on their way to Egypt. Then the brothers put goat's blood on Joseph's special coat and showed it to their father. How sad Jacob was! He believed that a wild animal had killed Joseph.

What did Joseph's brothers do to him? What do you think they told their father? GENESIS 37

Joseph Works Hard

Joseph was sold to a man in Egypt named Potiphar. Joseph became his slave. God helped Joseph to work hard. His master was pleased with him and put him in charge of all of his other slaves.

After a while, Potiphar's wife wanted Joseph to do something very wrong. When Joseph said no, she decided to get even with him. So she told her husband a lie about Joseph. She told him that Joseph had tried to hurt her. Potiphar believed her and put Joseph in jail!

But God took care of Joseph. God made the man in charge of the jail feel friendly toward Joseph. The man put Joseph in charge of all the other prisoners.

Even though Joseph didn't want to be a slave, he worked hard to be a good one. Do you have a chore that you don't like to do? How can you do your very best job in doing it? GENESIS 39

Joseph Is Put in Charge

One night, Pharaoh of Egypt had two strange dreams. These dreams bothered the king very much. He sent for all his wise men, but they couldn't tell him what his dreams meant. Then Pharaoh sent for Joseph. He had heard that Joseph could tell what dreams meant. But Joseph told Pharaoh that it was God who would show him the meaning of the dreams. Here is what God showed Joseph: there would be seven years of good crops in Egypt, with plenty to eat. Then there would be seven years of poor crops, and everyone would be hungry. Joseph told Pharaoh to put someone in charge and make the people save up grain during the good years so there would be enough food for the bad years. Pharaoh thought this was a good idea, and he put Joseph in charge!

Joseph knew he couldn't help Pharaoh without God's help. What is one thing you can ask God to help you with today? GENESIS 40–41

Joseph Meets His Brothers

Joseph was now a very important man in Egypt. He was in charge of saving up all the extra grain during the seven years of good crops. When the seven years of poor crops came, Joseph had plenty of grain for all the people of Egypt and for others, too.

Joseph's father and brothers heard about the food in Egypt. So all the brothers went to Egypt to buy some. When they bowed down in front of him to ask for food, Joseph remembered his dreams from a long time ago. They had come true!

Joseph's brothers didn't recognize him because he was grown up now. So Joseph pretended that he thought they were enemy spies. He did this so he could find out if his brothers were better men than they used to be. Joseph told them he was

going to keep Benjamin as a slave. The brothers begged him to keep them instead of Benjamin because their father loved Benjamin  so much. They told each other that God was punishing them for selling Joseph. When Joseph realized how sorry they were for what they had done to him, he told his brothers, "I am Joseph!" How excited and happy they all were that Joseph was alive and had forgiven them!

Is there someone whom you need to forgive? Be like Joseph and tell that person you forgive him or her. GENESIS 42–43

A Princess Finds A Baby

Jacob and his sons and their families moved to Egypt to live near Joseph. After hundreds of years, their children and grandchildren and their grandchildren's children became a great nation.

Then a new king began to rule over Egypt who didn't care about what Joseph had done to save Egypt. This Pharaoh was afraid of Jacob's family (now called Israelites) because there were so many of them. So he made them all slaves. He also tried to kill all the Israelite boys as soon as they were born so they wouldn't fight against him when they grew up.

There was one Israelite baby boy named Moses. His mother put him in a basket

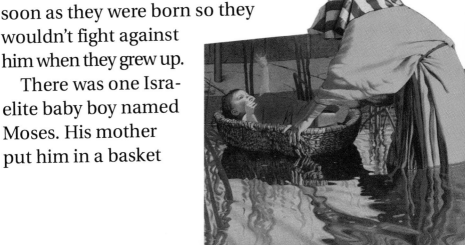

and hid it in the bushes by the river because she was afraid Pharaoh would come and kill him. Moses' sister, Miriam, hid nearby to watch over him.

Soon Pharaoh's daughter came down to the river to take a bath. She found Moses crying in the basket and felt sorry for him, so she decided to adopt him as her own son! Miriam came out of the bushes and asked, "May I go and get a woman to take care of the baby for you?" The princess said yes, and Miriam ran home and got her mother. The princess told Moses' mother she would pay her to take care of the baby until he was old enough to come and live as her son in the palace.

Do you think Moses' mother asked God to keep her baby safe? How did God take care of Moses? How does he take care of you? EXODUS 1–2

God Asks Moses to Help Him

One day when Moses was grown-up, he saw an Egyptian hitting an Israelite. This made Moses very angry, and he killed the Egyptian and hid his body in the sand. The king heard about what Moses had done and tried to arrest him. But Moses ran far away to the land of Midian, where

the king couldn't find him. He became a shepherd and lived there for many years.

One day when Moses was out taking care of
the sheep, he saw a strange thing. He saw a bush
on fire, but the bush didn't burn up.

Just then God called to him from the bush. "Moses! Moses!"

Just imagine how surprised and frightened Moses was, but he said, "Yes, Lord, I'm listening."

Then God told Moses he had heard the unhappy cries of the Israelite slaves in Egypt. God told Moses to go to Pharaoh and tell him to stop hurting the Israelites and to let them leave Egypt and go back to Canaan. But Moses was afraid to go; he was afraid Pharaoh would hurt or kill him if he told him to let the Israelites go.

"I will be with you and help you," God told Moses. And God sent Moses' brother, Aaron, to help him.

What did God tell Moses to do? Why didn't Moses need to be afraid to talk to Pharaoh?
EXODUS 2–4

Pharaoh Doesn't Listen

Moses and Aaron went to Egypt. They told Pharaoh, "The Lord God of Israel says,'Let my people leave Egypt and worship me in the desert.'"

But Pharaoh didn't believe in God, and he wouldn't let the Israelites go. Instead, he made them work even harder. Then God did an amazing thing. He turned Aaron's shepherd rod into a snake. When Pharaoh's magicians made snakes too, Aaron's snake ate those snakes up. But even after seeing this, Pharaoh would not listen to Moses.

The next day, Moses again told Pharaoh to let the Israelites go. Again, Pharaoh wouldn't listen. Then Aaron touched the Nile River with his rod, and God turned all the water in Egypt into blood. No one could drink it, and all the fish died. Still, Pharaoh would not let the people go.

Why wouldn't Pharaoh listen to Moses and Aaron? What was one of the amazing things God did? EXODUS 5–7

Pharaoh Sees God's Power

Pharaoh would not let the Israelites leave Egypt to worship God, so God sent millions of frogs to cover the land. There were frogs everywhere! Pharaoh told Moses he would let the Israelites go if Moses prayed to God to take the frogs away. Moses did this. But when Pharaoh saw all the frogs die, he changed his mind and would not let the people go.

Then God changed the dust on the ground into millions of small insects called lice that covered the people and the cattle. When Pharaoh still would not listen, God sent mil-

lions of flies. They swarmed over everything,
except the part of the country where the Israelites lived. Pharaoh hated the flies and promised
to let the Israelites go, but when God took the
flies away, Pharaoh broke his promise and would
not let them go. So God sent a terrible sickness
that killed many of the Egyptians' animals. Then
terrible sores broke out all over the Egyptians

and their animals. Then hail and fire fell out of the sky, killing the Egyptians' animals out in the fields and destroying their crops. When Pharaoh still wouldn't listen, God sent insects called locusts to eat up all the gardens and crops that were still left. Then God covered the land of the Egyptians with darkness for three days, but the land where the Israelites lived was not dark at all.

Pharaoh's heart was very bad. He pretended to change his mind each time God sent troubles to Egypt, but when they stopped, he still would not let the Israelites leave.

Pharaoh was a stubborn man. He thought he was bigger than God. What do you think? Name three things God did to show how powerful he is.
EXODUS 8–11

The Israelites Leave Egypt

Moses became very angry at Pharaoh for not obeying God. He told Pharaoh that God was going to send one last, terrible punishment. God himself would come to Egypt one night and cause the oldest son in every Egyptian home to die—even Pharaoh's son

would die! But not one of the Israelite children would be hurt. Then Moses went to the Israelite people and told them to prepare to leave Egypt in four days. He told them that on the fourth day, each family was to kill a lamb and eat the meat for dinner. They were to put its blood on each side of their door and up above it too. When the Lord came that night, he would pass over each home that had blood on the door, but where there wasn't any blood on the door, he would kill the oldest son.

At last that terrible night came. God saw the blood on the Israelites' doors and passed over their homes. And the meal they ate that night became known as the *Passover* because God "passed over" their homes. But God went into every Egyptian home that did not have blood on the door and killed the oldest son. Oh, how the Egyptians cried! Then Pharaoh called Moses and told him, "Take your people and all their belongings and leave Egypt now!"

The Israelites were ready. They took all their belongings and animals as well as the clothes, gold, and silver that the Egyptians gave them as they left Egypt. And God showed them the way through the desert. During the day he went in front of them in a cloud shaped like a pillar. At night the cloud became a pillar of fire that gave them light.

Why did the Israelites put lamb's blood on their doors? What is the name of the special meal they ate? EXODUS 11–13

Crossing the Red Sea

Soon after the Israelites left Egypt, Pharaoh was sorry he let them go. He and his army got into their chariots and chased after them. They caught up with God's people by the Red Sea.

The Israelites were frightened and cried out to God to save them. "This is your fault, Moses," they whined. But before the Egyptian army could

reach them, God moved the pillar of cloud between the Egyptians and the Israelites, so the Egyptians couldn't find God's people!

"Hold out your rod over the sea," God told Moses. Moses held out his rod, and the water opened up in front of them, making a path across the bottom of the sea. Moses and the Israelites walked safely to the other side on dry ground. When the Egyptian chariots tried to go after them, God told Moses to hold out his rod again. Then the water came crashing down upon the Egyptian army, and all of them were drowned.

God helped the Israelites, and he can help you, too. Do you need God's help this week? Don't wait any longer to ask for his help. EXODUS 14

God Sends Food

The Israelites began to travel across a huge desert to the land God had promised them. But there was not enough food, and they started to complain angrily. They blamed Moses and Aaron for bringing them out into the desert. "We would rather be slaves back in Egypt!" they shouted.

God heard their complaints. He told Moses that he would send food, and God kept his promise! In the evenings, huge flocks of birds called quail flew into the Israelites' camp. The people were able to catch them and cook them for their meals. In the mornings, the ground was covered with flakes of bread. The people called it *manna*, which means "what is it?" God told the people to collect just

enough manna for
each day, no more. However, on
the day before each Sabbath, they
were to collect enough for two days
because God wanted them to rest on the Sabbath. He didn't want them to work by picking up
manna that day.

Can you name some foods to thank God for?
Did you know that all your food comes from God?
Remember to thank him at each meal. EXODUS 16

God's Commandments

God called Moses to come up to the top of a mountain called Sinai. There God wrote these ten commandments on stone tablets and gave them to Moses. These commandments are for everyone.

1. Do not worship any god but me. You must not make any idols. We must love God more than anything or anyone else.

2. Do not take the Lord's name in vain. Always use God's name with love and affection.

3. Remember to observe the Sabbath as a holy day. On Sunday let us worship God and thank him for his gifts. Just as God rested on the Sabbath, we should relax on Sunday.

4. Honor your father and your mother. Respect, love, and obey your parents.

5. You must not kill. We shouldn't even wish

that some-
one would die.
We must overcome
anger and hatred in
our hearts for others.

6. *You must not commit adultery.* It is wrong for
a man to pretend that a woman is his wife when
he is married to someone else. And it is wrong for
a woman to pretend that a man is her husband
when she is married to someone else. God wants
husbands and wives to be absolutely faithful to
each other.

7. *You must not steal.* We must not take anything that belongs to someone else.

8. *You must not tell lies.* We must never say anything that is not true.

9. *You must not desire your neighbor's wife.* Hus-

bands and wives should desire and love only each other and not do anything to harm that love.

10. You must not envy and desire your neighbor's goods. We must not be jealous of what others have.

God gave these commandments to help you. What happens when you don't obey these commandments? Who can help you obey them? EXODUS 19–20

Aaron Makes an Idol

While God was speaking to Moses on the mountain, the Israelites got tired of waiting for him to return, and they did a very bad thing. They decided to make an idol and worship it. An idol is a statue of an animal, a person, or a bird. The people asked Moses' brother, Aaron, to make them a statue of a calf. They gave Aaron their gold jewelry, and he melted it in a fire and shaped the gold into the form of a calf. Then the people bowed

to the gold calf and said it was their god who had brought them out of Egypt. The people had a wild party, feasting and getting drunk and dancing around the calf-idol.

Then Moses came down the mountain and saw what the people were doing.,Angrily he threw down the stone tablets with the Ten Commandments on them, and they broke in pieces. Then he smashed the idol and ground it into powder. Then he threw the powder into the water and made the people drink it.

God was very angry with the people too. But Moses begged God to forgive them, and God listened to Moses.

Did the gold calf bring the Israelites safely out of Egypt? Who did? Why do you think the Israelites did this foolish thing? EXODUS 32

God Punishes His People

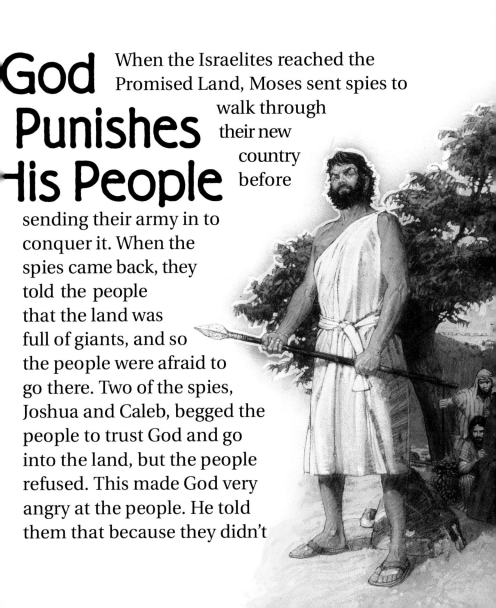

When the Israelites reached the Promised Land, Moses sent spies to walk through their new country before sending their army in to conquer it. When the spies came back, they told the people that the land was full of giants, and so the people were afraid to go there. Two of the spies, Joshua and Caleb, begged the people to trust God and go into the land, but the people refused. This made God very angry at the people. He told them that because they didn't trust him, they would wander in the wilderness for forty years before they could enter the Promised Land. Oh, how sorry the people were then!

While they were in the wilderness, the Israelites began to complain again because they had no water. Then God told Moses to speak to a certain rock and water would pour out of it. But Moses was angry at the people because of their complaining. "Must I bring you water from the rock?" he demanded. He was acting big and saying that he, instead of God, would do this miracle. And then, instead of speaking to the rock as God had told him to, he hit it twice with his rod. Water gushed out, just like God had promised. But Moses had not obeyed God. He had hit the rock instead of speaking to it. So, God punished Moses by not letting him enter the Promised Land. How sad Moses was that he had disobeyed!

What did Moses do wrong? How did God punish him? NUMBERS 13–14; 20

GOD LEADS THE ISRAELITES TO CANAAN

God led the Israelites out of Egypt and to the Promised Land of Canaan. Can you find the Red Sea, where God opened up the water so the people could cross to the other side? Do you see Mount Sinai, where God gave the Israelites ten commandments to obey? Because the Israelites disobeyed God, they had to live in the wilderness for forty years before God would let them live in Canaan. But God took care of them and made them into a great nation.

GOSHEN

EGYPT

Nile River

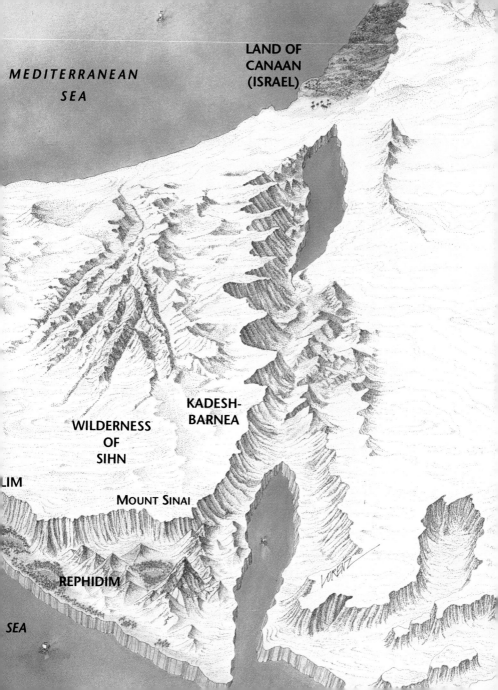

MEDITERRANEAN
SEA

LAND OF
CANAAN
(ISRAEL)

WILDERNESS
OF
SIHN

KADESH-
BARNEA

LIM

MOUNT SINAI

REPHIDIM

SEA

The Bronze Snake

Once again the Israelites sinned by complaining. "We don't have water," they whined. "We're tired of traveling, and we hate the food God gives us!" God was angry and sent snakes into the camp to bite the people, and many of them died. The people ran to Moses, screaming, "We have sinned! Please pray that the snakes will go away!" Moses prayed for them. Then God told Moses to make a bronze snake and put it on a pole. If people bitten by the snakes simply looked at the bronze snake, they would get well again. So Moses put a bronze snake on a pole, and many people looked at it and lived instead of dying from their snakebites.

The snake lifted up on a pole reminds us of someone in the Bible who was lifted up on a cross and died for our sins. Do you know his name? (His name is Jesus. He is God's own Son.) NUMBERS 21

86

Balaam's Donkey Speaks

King Balak of Moab sent for Balaam, a prophet of God, offering him money if he would ask God to send some great evil on the Israelites. Because Balaam loved money, he agreed to do this bad thing and started down the road on his donkey to do it. This made God angry, and he sent an angel with a sword to stand in the road and kill him. Balaam couldn't see the angel, but his donkey could. When the donkey went off the road to keep away from the angel, Balaam

beat her for misbehaving. Then God made the donkey speak. "Why are you beating me?" she asked. Then God opened Balaam's eyes, and he saw the angel and was frightened. God told Balaam to bless the Israelites and not curse them.

Why did the donkey go off the road? What did the donkey say to Balaam?
NUMBERS 22–24

Rahab and the Spies

While the Israelites were still in the wilderness, Moses died.

Then God said to Joshua, "You must lead the Israelites across the Jordan River into the Promised Land. Do not be afraid. I will be with you."

While the Israelites were getting ready to go, Joshua sent two spies across the river to spy on the city of Jericho. There they met a woman named Rahab who knew that God was helping the Israelites. When the king of Jericho sent his soldiers to capture the spies, Rahab hid them on her roof under some straw until the soldiers left. Then she helped the two men climb down a rope on the outside of the city wall. Before they left, she asked them not to hurt her family when they attacked the city. The spies promised not to. They told her to hang a red rope from the window of her house so they would recognize it

again. Then they returned to Joshua and told him all that had happened.

How did the spies get out of the city? What did the spies promise Rahab? JOSHUA 1–2

Crossing the Jordan River

Joshua and all the people got up early the next morning and traveled to the Jordan River. They camped beside it for three days. Then Joshua told the people to get ready to cross the river. God was going to do a great miracle, and they would walk across on dry ground!

The priests went first, carrying the ark of the covenant, the special box that held the Ten Commandments. As soon as the priests' feet touched the water, the water dried up in front of them, and all the people walked across on dry ground! The priests built a stone monument in the middle of the river so that everyone who saw it would remember what God had done for his people. Then, when everyone had gone across, the priests carried the ark out of the river, and the water began flowing again.

How did the people get across the river? What do we call it when God does something that no one else can do? (We call it a miracle. Did you get the right answer?) JOSHUA 3–4

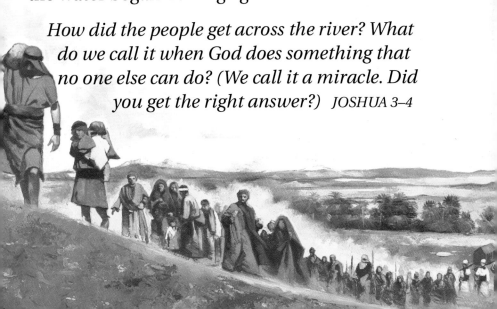

The Battle of Jericho

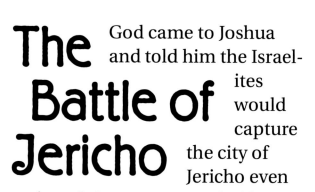

God came to Joshua and told him the Israelites would capture the city of Jericho even though it was surrounded by high walls. Jericho was part of the Promised Land that God was giving to his people.

God told Joshua how to plan his attack. He said that all the Israelite soldiers must march around the city once each day for six days; and the priests must go with them carrying the ark of the covenant. Seven priests were to go ahead of the ark and blow trumpets. On the seventh day, they were to march around Jericho—not once, but seven times. At the end of the seventh time around, the priests were to blow one loud trumpet blast, and the army was to give a mighty shout. Then the walls of the city would fall down flat, and the Israelites could walk right in!

So the Israelite army did as God commanded. Once each day, for six days, they marched around the city. And on the seventh day, after marching seven times around the walls, they blew the trumpets, the people shouted, and the walls came crashing down! Then the Israelites rushed into Jericho and captured it.

But Rahab and her family were not hurt, just as the Israelite spies had promised.

God kept his promise to help his people. The spies kept their promise to protect Rahab and her family. What is a promise you've made that you can keep today? JOSHUA 5–6

The Sun and Moon Stand Still

God was with the Israelites and helped them capture many cities in the Promised Land. But the people in the city of Gibeon tricked the Israelites into making a peace treaty with them instead of destroying them. A peace treaty means that the Israelites and the Gibeonites promised to help, not hurt, each other. And the Israelites did not want to break their promise.

But this peace treaty made the other kings in the land angry at the Gibeonites. Five kings and their armies got together and attacked Gibeon. The Gibeonites were afraid and sent a messenger to Joshua, saying, "Quick! Keep your promise. Come and help us!"

So Joshua and his army fought against the other armies. The Lord made the other armies

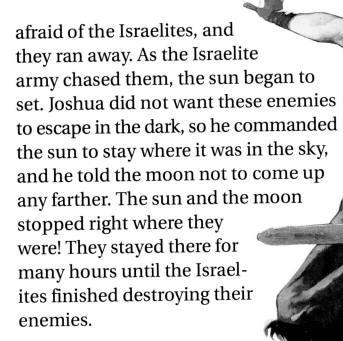

afraid of the Israelites, and they ran away. As the Israelite army chased them, the sun began to set. Joshua did not want these enemies to escape in the dark, so he commanded the sun to stay where it was in the sky, and he told the moon not to come up any farther. The sun and the moon stopped right where they were! They stayed there for many hours until the Israelites finished destroying their enemies.

Who made the sun and the moon (see Genesis 1)? Who do you think stopped them from moving? JOSHUA 9–10

Gideon's Little Army

God told the Israelites to chase from the land all the people who prayed to idols instead of praying to God. But rather than obeying God, many Israelites married these people and started worshiping their idols. This made God sad and angry. So he allowed some enemies to capture the Israelites and make them slaves. Then the people cried out to God to help them.

One day God came in the form of an angel to a man named Gideon. The angel told him, "I have chosen you to free the Israelites from their enemies. I will help you."

Gideon wanted to be sure it was God who had made this promise, so he asked him to do a miracle. This is the miracle Gideon asked God to do: Gideon said he would leave some wool outside all night. In the morning, if the wool was wet with dew and the ground was dry, he would know God was going to help him.

So Gideon left some wool out all night. In the morning, the wool was wet with dew, but the ground around it was dry. Then, the next night, Gideon asked God to keep the wool dry even though the ground was wet, and God did! When Gideon saw these miracles, he knew it was God who had made the promise.

Gideon gathered the Israelite men together to fight against the huge enemy army. But God told him, "You have too many men!" God told Gideon to pick only three hundred men to fight in his army. How could they win with so few?

But Gideon trusted God to help them. He gave each of his men a trumpet and a clay pot with a lighted lamp inside. He told his men that when they came to the enemy camp, they should blow their trumpets, break their clay pots, and shout, "The sword of the Lord and of Gideon!"

And that is just what they did. When the enemy soldiers heard the noise and saw the burning lamps that had been hidden in the pots, they yelled in fear and ran for their lives.

What miracles did God do?
JUDGES 6–7

Samson's Great Strength

Again, the Israelites sinned by worshiping idols. And again, God allowed them to be captured and become slaves.

One day God sent an angel to a man named Manoah. The angel told Manoah and his wife they were going to have a baby boy. When he grew up, their son would free the Israelites from being slaves. To show he was special, he must never drink wine or cut his hair. If he followed these instructions, then God would be with him.

When the baby was born several months later, they named him Samson. He grew up and became a very strong man. Samson never drank wine, and he never cut his hair. One day, a young lion attacked Samson, and God gave him the strength to kill it with his bare hands! Another time, when some enemies tried to trap him by closing the city gates, Samson picked up the huge gates and carried them away.

Samson obeyed God, and God helped him. You and I must obey God, too, and then he will help us.

JUDGES 13–14; 16

Samson Is Captured

God gave Samson great strength so he could fight God's enemies. One day the enemy army came to capture him. But Samson picked up a bone he found beside the road and killed a thousand enemy soldiers with it.

Samson had a girlfriend named Delilah who was the daughter of one of the enemy soldiers. Samson's enemies offered to give money to Delilah if she would find out how to make Samson weak so they could capture him. But when Delilah asked Samson what would make him weak, he lied to her. He told her if she tied him with seven ropes made of green flax, he would be as weak as other men.

After Samson fell asleep, Delilah tied him up with seven ropes of green flax. Then she cried out, "Samson, your enemies are here to get you!"

But Samson jumped up and easily broke the ropes.

Delilah pouted because Samson hadn't told her the truth. Again she begged him to tell her his secret. Finally, Samson told her. If his hair were cut, he would no longer be strong.

When Samson fell asleep, Delilah cut off his long hair. "Samson," she cried out, "your enemies are here to get you!"

Now Samson was as weak as other men. God had left him. So his enemies put chains on him, poked out his eyes so that he was blind, and put him in prison.

One day Samson's enemies were having a huge party inside their temple. "Send for Samson so we

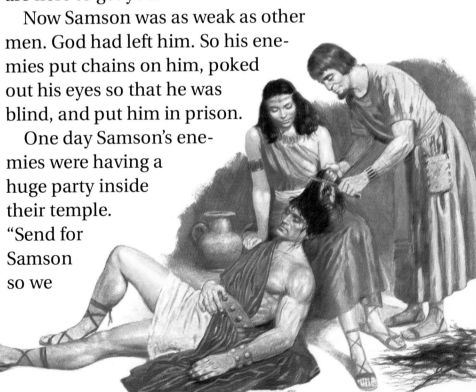

can tease him," someone suggested. So they brought out blind Samson and stood him between two giant pillars that held up the temple.

Samson asked God to give him strength just one more time. Then he pushed on the pillars, and the stone roof came crashing down on Samson and all his enemies. Samson died that day, but the enemy kings and thousands of enemy people were killed, too.

Was Delilah a good friend to Samson? If you pick friends who don't care about God, they can make you forget about doing what is right. Pick your friends more carefully than Samson did.

JUDGES 15–16

Unselfish Ruth

An Israelite woman named Naomi, who had moved away from the land of Israel, decided to return there after her husband and sons died. They had lived in the faraway land of Moab for many years. Ruth, one of her Moabite daughters-in-law, told her, "I will go with you. Your God will be my God." So Ruth left her friends and went with Naomi to Canaan. Because they were very poor, Ruth went out into a neighbor's field to gather the grain that the workers dropped while they were harvesting. People who were poor were allowed to get food this way. Boaz, the kind owner of the field, saw Ruth and heard about how she was helping Naomi. He told his workers to drop extra grain for her. Then Boaz told Ruth he would marry her and take care of her and Naomi!

In what way was Ruth unselfish? What is something you can do today that is unselfish? RUTH

God Speaks to Samuel

Hannah was unhappy because she didn't have any children. One day Hannah went to God's house to pray. She promised God that if he would give her a son, she would give him back to God to be a helper in God's house.

God answered Hannah's prayer and gave her a son. Hannah named him Samuel. But she didn't forget her promise. While Samuel was still a little boy, Hannah brought him to God's house to live with Eli, the priest, and to be his helper.

One night after Samuel had gone to bed, he heard a voice calling him. He ran to Eli. "What do you want, Eli?" he asked.

But Eli said he hadn't called him, so Samuel went back to bed. Samuel heard the voice two more times, but each time Eli told him he hadn't called him. Then Eli knew it was God who was

calling Samuel. Eli told Samuel, "If he calls you again, say, 'Speak, Lord, I am listening.'"

So Samuel went back to bed. Then God called him again. "Yes, Lord," Samuel answered. "Speak, for I am listening."

Then God gave Samuel an important message for Eli. Samuel was a good listener and gave God's message to Eli.

God wants to talk to you like he did to Samuel. You won't hear his voice, but he will talk to you when you read your Bible. 1 SAMUEL 1; 3

The Ark Is Captured

One day the men of Israel went out to fight against their enemies, and four thousand Israelite soldiers died. The leaders of Israel wondered why God had allowed so many to be killed. They decided to carry God's special gold chest with the Ten Commandments in it, called the ark of the covenant, into battle with them. They thought carrying this special box with them would make God help them.

But that was their own idea, not God's. When the enemy army attacked, it killed thirty thousand Israelites and captured the ark!

The enemy soldiers put the ark inside the temple of their idol. But when they came back to the temple, the idol had fallen on its face on the floor beside the ark. They set up the idol, but that night it again fell down in front of the ark. This

time its head and hands were cut off! Then a terrible sickness came upon the enemy. God was punishing them for taking the ark. Finally they put the ark in a wagon pulled by two cows, and, all by themselves, the cows took it back to the Israelites.

Why do you think the enemy's idol fell over? How did God punish the enemy? 1 SAMUEL 4–6

Jonathan's Brave Fight

The people of Israel wanted a king like other nations had. God already was their king, so it was wrong of them to want another one. God warned the people that a king would bring trouble, but the people wouldn't listen. So God picked out a man named Saul to be their king. Saul was good-looking and strong. He looked like a king.

Saul helped the Israelites win many battles. But one day they had to fight a huge enemy army. There were so many enemy soldiers that no one could count them. The Israelite soldiers were scared. They hid in caves and would not fight. But Saul's son Jonathan and one other soldier trusted God to take care of them. They climbed a steep hill to where some enemy soldiers were and killed twenty of them. Then God sent an earthquake. The ground shook and all

the enemy
soldiers ran
away.

*Are you
ever afraid
of something
or someone?
Ask God to
help you.
He will!*
1 SAMUEL 8–11;

13–14

God Chooses a New King

Samuel was an old man now. He had brought God's messages to the Israelites for many years. Now he brought a message to King Saul. Samuel told Saul that God was unhappy because Saul had stopped being a good king and had disobeyed God's commands. Samuel told Saul that someday soon he would no longer be king. God had chosen a new king for Israel.

Then God sent Samuel to a man named Jesse who had many sons. Samuel thought God might pick one of the older sons to be the new king. But God chose the youngest son, David, who was just a shepherd boy. Samuel took a bottle of olive oil and poured the oil on David's head. This was to show that he would be the next king, but not until after King Saul was dead. Then God sent his Holy Spirit into David's heart to make him wise

and good. But God took his Spirit away from King Saul.

Think of one thing God wants you to do. Does he want you to be nice to someone who is unkind? Does he want you to obey your parents without complaining? It doesn't matter how young you are, God will help you do it. Ask him.

1 SAMUEL 15–16

David Fights Goliath

Once again the enemy decided to fight Israel, and King Saul and his army got ready for battle. The enemy army was on one mountain, and the Israelite army was on another mountain. The two were separated by a valley.

One of the enemy soldiers was a giant named Goliath. He marched around in the valley between the two armies and yelled to the army of Israel, "I'll fight the best man in your army. If he can kill me, my soldiers will be your slaves; but if I kill him, then you must be our slaves!"

Every day for forty days, Goliath shouted at the Israelites. But Saul and the Israelite soldiers were frightened; no one wanted to fight Goliath.

One day Jesse's son David came to the Israelites' camp. His father had sent him with food for his older brothers who were soldiers. When

David heard Goliath's shouting and saw how frightened the Israelites were, he told King Saul, "I would like to fight Goliath."

"But you're only a boy," Saul said. "You can't beat this giant!"

"Yes I can," David replied. "Once I killed a lion who was hurting my sheep. Another time I killed a bear with my bare hands. God will help me kill this bad giant just like he helped me kill the lion and the bear."

So David took his shepherd's stick and his sling, and picking up five smooth stones, he went into the valley to fight Goliath.

"Come over here so I can kill you," shouted Goliath.

David answered him, "You trust in your sword and your armor, but I trust in God."

When Goliath came closer, David put a stone in his sling and sent it sailing toward

Goliath. It hit him in the middle of his forehead, and he fell down dead. Then David ran over to him and used Goliath's own sword to cut off his head.

When the enemy soldiers saw that Goliath was dead, they ran away. Then the Israelites chased after them, killing many of them.

Why were the Israelites afraid? Why wasn't David afraid to fight Goliath? 1 SAMUEL 17

David's Friend Jonathan

After the Israelites had chased the enemy army away, the captain of the Israelite army brought David to King Saul. Saul's son Jonathan was there. When Jonathan saw David and heard him speaking with his father, he loved him as if he were his brother. Jonathan was David's friend from then on, and he and David promised always to be kind to each other. To show that he meant to keep his promise, Jonathan gave David his robe, sword, bow, and belt. Then King Saul made David a commander in his army.

As King Saul, David, Jonathan, and the Israelite soldiers traveled home, people came out of their homes along the way and cheered. The people sang and danced for joy. This was their song: "Saul has killed his thousands, and David his ten thousands!" The people were saying that David was a better soldier than King Saul was. This made Saul angry. From then on he was jealous of David and wanted to get rid of him.

What did Jonathan give David to show his friendship? Why was Saul jealous of David?

1 SAMUEL 18

Saul Is Jealous

An evil spirit had come into King Saul's heart. When the evil spirit made Saul act crazy, David played beautiful music on his harp to calm him. But even though David was kind, King Saul was jealous of David. He could see that God was with David and helping him.

One day Saul threw a spear at David. He

wanted to kill David. But David
jumped out of the way just in time. Then King
Saul began to hate David.

King Saul's son Jonathan begged his father not
to hurt David, and for a little while the king listened to Jonathan. But when David helped the
army win another battle, King Saul again tried to
kill him. Then David ran away.

*Are you jealous of someone? Stop! Ask God to
take your jealousy away before you do something
foolish like King Saul did.*   1 SAMUEL 18–19

David Doesn't Get Even

David ran to the wilderness and hid in a cave. King Saul chased after him with his army, but God kept David safe. One day the king went alone into a cave. He didn't know that David and some of his friends were hiding there. David's men wanted to kill the king, but David wouldn't let them. Instead, David sneaked up behind King Saul and cut off a piece of his robe. When the king left the cave, David called out to him, "See this piece of your robe! I could have killed you. But that is not what God wants. He is the one who will punish you if you are wrong!"

Then King Saul was sorry he had tried to kill David, and he stopped chasing him and went home.

What could David have done? Why didn't he?

1 SAMUEL 23–24

130

David Takes Saul's Spear

King Saul was afraid that the people wanted to make David their king instead of him, so he and his army started to chase after David again.

While Saul and his army were camping near David's hiding place, David and his nephew Abishai crept into their camp at night. They found Saul and his soldiers asleep. Abishai wanted to kill Saul, but David wouldn't let him. "It isn't right to kill the king God gave us," David told him. Instead, they took Saul's spear and his water jug. When they were a safe distance away, David shouted and woke up the king. "See, I have taken your spear and your water jug. I was close enough to kill you, but I didn't!"

Then the king was sorry for what he had done. He promised David he wouldn't try to hurt him again.

132

Should David believe King Saul's promise? If you tell lies, do you think people will trust you? *1 SAMUEL 26*

Saul Visits a Witch

The enemy army decided to attack King Saul and the Israelites again. There were so many enemy soldiers that King Saul was very frightened. He asked God what he should do, but God would not answer him. So the king asked a witch for help. He told this witch to call up the spirit of Samuel, who was now dead. This was very wrong of Saul. God had commanded that anyone who called up spirits should be killed.

When Samuel's ghost appeared, he told Saul that because he had disobeyed God again and again, God was no longer with him. Samuel told him that the next day the enemy army would destroy the whole Israelite army. King Saul and Jonathan would die too. Then David would become the new king.

King Saul was so frightened when he heard this that he fell facedown on the ground.

King Saul kept disobeying God, so now God didn't answer him and wouldn't tell him what to do. You and I must be careful to obey God. Then he can help us. *1 SAMUEL 28*

King Saul Dies

The next day the enemy army attacked the Israelite army. Frightened, the Israelites ran from them. But King Saul was badly wounded by an arrow and couldn't get away. He groaned and told the soldier who was with him, "Kill me. If our enemies capture me, they will torture me." But the soldier was afraid to kill his king. So King Saul killed himself with his own sword. When the soldier saw that the king was dead, he killed himself too. Many Israelites died that day, including King Saul's son Jonathan. The enemy won the battle, as Samuel had told King Saul they would.

Then the people of Israel made David their king, and he helped them win many battles. He

became a very great man, for God helped him in everything.

The soldier refused to obey Saul because murder is a sin. We should never sin, even if someone important tells us to do it.
1 SAMUEL 29; 31; 2 SAMUEL 5

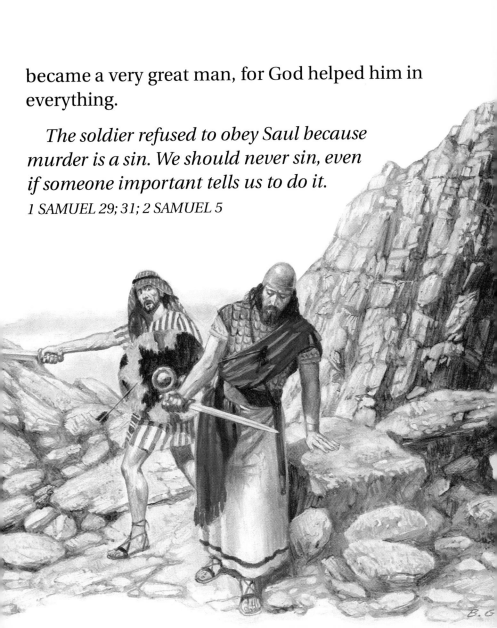

The Ark Comes Home

Do you remember when the enemy captured God's special gold chest, called the ark of the covenant? When they sent it back to Israel, it had been put in the house of a man named Abinadab. It had stayed there for twenty years while Saul was the king, because he didn't care about it. But now King

David wanted to bring the ark to the city of Jerusalem. The priests brought the ark to Jerusalem with joyful shouts and music. David was so happy that he jumped and danced for joy. The priests put the ark in the special tent-house David had made for it. Then David offered sacrifices to God and gave the people gifts.

Why did David leap and dance? Do you remember why the ark was so special? 2 SAMUEL 6–7

David Fights His Son

King David had a son named Absalom. Absalom had long hair and was very handsome. He also was very proud. He was so proud that he thought he should be king instead of his father. So Absalom got his many friends to call him their king, and then he led them to Jerusalem to kill King David! But King David and his men got out of Jerusalem before Absalom arrived.

Absalom and his army didn't give up. They chased King David. Finally, the two armies fought, and God helped David's side win. But it was a sad day because twenty thousand men died in the battle.

During the battle, Absalom rode his donkey under a tree, and his long hair got caught in a tree branch. He was stuck and couldn't get away. One of David's generals came up to Absalom and

killed him, even though David had told him not
to. When David heard that his son was dead, he
started to weep. "Oh, Absalom, my son, my son!"
he cried.

*Absalom's pride hurt many people. When we
are proud and selfish, we hurt others too. A proud
heart is a sinful heart.* 2 SAMUEL 14–18

King Solomon's Wisdom

The years went by, and King David grew old. Before he died, he made his son Solomon the new king. He told Solomon, "Obey God and worship him with all your heart."

Solomon listened to his father and was careful to do what was right. One night God spoke to him and told him he could have anything he wanted! Solomon decided to ask for wisdom. He wanted always to know what would help his people the most. Solomon's request pleased God. So God made him very rich as well as very wise.

One day two women came to Solomon with a problem. Each said she was the mother of the same baby. This could not be, but how could Solomon know who was telling the truth? Solomon told his soldier, "Cut the baby in two pieces and give half to each woman!"

One of the women said, "Yes, cut the baby in
half."

But the other woman cried out, "Don't kill him!
Give her the child." For she loved her baby very
much and didn't want him to die.

Then wise Solomon said, "Give the baby to the
woman who wants him to live. She is his mother."

*What did Solomon wish for? How did he an-
swer the two mothers with the baby? Do you think
his decision was a wise one?* 1 KINGS 1–3

God's Temple Is Built

God had given Solomon instructions to build a beautiful temple where the Israelites could worship God. So Solomon sent many men to cut down the best cedar trees for wood to build with. And he had the best workmen make beautiful things for the temple from gold, silver, bronze, iron, and wood, and from expensive cloth.

It took Solomon and his workmen seven years to complete the temple. The walls inside were covered with gold, and so was the floor, and there were beautiful carvings and jewels in many places. There also was a special inner room called the Most Holy Place where the ark of the covenant was to be kept.

How did Solomon know how to build the temple? Where in the temple was the ark placed?
1 KINGS 5–7

King Solomon Sins

A queen of a faraway country heard of King Solomon's wisdom and riches. She came to visit him and brought him gifts of expensive spices and gold and precious stones. She was amazed by the beauty of his palace and of God's temple. She asked Solomon hard questions and heard his wise answers. "You are even wiser and richer than I was told!" she exclaimed.

But as Solomon grew older, he began to disobey God. He married many beautiful women who worshiped idols instead of God. Soon Solomon was worshiping the idols too.

God was angry with Solomon because he worshiped idols. God said that because Solomon had done these things, his son could not be king when Solomon died. His son would rule only part of the kingdom.

And that is just what happened. After Solomon

died, his son became ruler over the southern part of the kingdom, which was called Judah. But the rest of the Israelites picked a different king to rule the northern part of the country, which they called Israel.

Solomon started out as a wise king, but he stopped being wise when he stopped putting God first. You are wise if you give your life to God. You are foolish if you don't. 1 KINGS 10–12

Ravens Feed Elijah

After Solomon died, many kings ruled the northern kingdom of Israel, and all of them were bad. But King Ahab was the worst. He married a woman who worshiped an idol. Then he built a temple for this idol and chose bad men as priests to offer sacrifices to the idol. Soon the people of Israel were worshiping this idol too. How sad and angry this made God.

God sent a prophet named Elijah to King Ahab. Elijah told the king, "Because of your sin, God will not send rain on the land of Israel for three years." This made King Ahab very angry, and he tried to kill Elijah, but God took care of his prophet. God told Elijah to hide beside a stream in the wilderness. While he was there, God commanded birds called ravens to bring food to him every morning and evening.

Why was Ahab angry? How did God take care of Elijah?
1 KINGS 16–17

Elijah's Contest

One day God told Elijah to find King Ahab and command him to come to Mount Carmel with his prophets and all the people. When they arrived there, Elijah asked them, "How long will it be before you decide if you will worship God or Ahab's idol?"

Then Elijah had a contest to show the people which was greater—God or Ahab's idol. He told the idol's prophets to place a sacrifice on their altar. But instead of lighting a fire, they were to pray to their idol to send fire and burn up the sacrifice. So they prayed and prayed. Then they yelled and screamed, but their idol did nothing.

Then Elijah placed his sacrifice on God's altar. He poured water on top of it and all around it. Then he prayed to God, and God sent fire from heaven! The fire burned up the sacrifice, the water, and even the stones of the altar!

What happened when the prophets prayed to the idol? What amazing thing happened when Elijah prayed to God?
1 KINGS 18

A Ride to Heaven

The day came when God decided to take Elijah up to heaven. Elijah's friend Elisha stayed close to the old prophet. He wanted to be with Elijah until God took him. Suddenly, a chariot and horses of fire swept between them and snatched Elijah away and took him up to heaven. Elisha never saw Elijah again on earth. He picked up Elijah's coat that had fallen on the ground. With the coat, Elisha struck the river he needed to cross. The water opened up before him, and he crossed over on dry ground.

What happened to the prophet Elijah? What amazing thing did Elisha do with Elijah's coat?
2 KINGS 2

Elisha Helps a Widow

One day a poor widow came to Elisha for help. She told Elisha that she owed some money and couldn't pay it back. The man to whom she owed the money said that if she didn't pay him, he would take her two sons and make them his slaves.

"Do you have anything you can sell?" Elisha asked her.

"Nothing except a small jar of olive oil," the widow told him.

Elisha told her to borrow empty jars from her neighbors and begin to pour her olive oil into them. So the woman borrowed jars from all her neighbors and brought them into her house and shut the door. Then she poured the olive oil into them from her one little jar, and the oil kept coming until all the jars were full! Then Elisha told her to sell the olive oil and pay the man what she owed him. She would even have extra money to buy food for her children.

God was able to do a wonderful thing for the woman because she did what God's prophet told her to do. God can do wonderful things for you when you obey him.

2 KINGS 4

Naaman Is Healed

A man named Naaman had a bad sickness called leprosy. It made his skin rot away. One day, a little Israelite slave girl told Naaman's wife about the prophet Elisha in Israel. She said Elisha could heal Naaman of his leprosy. So Naaman went to see Elisha. But when he came to Elisha's house, Elisha wouldn't even come to the door to see him. He just sent Naaman this message: "Go and wash yourself seven times in the Jordan River, and you will be healed."

At first Naaman was angry that Elisha wouldn't even come outside and pray for him. But Naaman's servants begged him to obey Elisha. So he went to the Jordan River and washed seven times. Suddenly, his skin was clean and healthy again. His leprosy was gone! Then Naaman knew Elisha's God was really God.

What did Elisha tell Naaman to do? What happened when Naaman obeyed Elisha? What would have happened if he hadn't obeyed? *2 KINGS 5*

Elisha's Fiery Army

An enemy army began to fight the Israelites. But Elisha warned the Israelite king that they were coming, and the Israelites escaped. This made the enemy soldiers very angry. They decided to capture Elisha and stop him from helping the Israelites. So one night they surrounded the city where Elisha was staying. Early the next morning, Elisha's servant saw enemy soldiers everywhere. He was very frightened. But Elisha told him, "Don't be afraid. We have more on our side than the enemy does!"

Then Elisha prayed that God would help his servant see better. Suddenly the servant could see a huge army of horses and chariots of fire in the hills surrounding the enemy army. Then God made the enemy army blind so they couldn't capture Elisha.

God is more powerful than the most powerful army. He can protect us no matter who tries to hurt us. *2 KINGS 6*

Joash Becomes King

King Ahaziah of Judah was a wicked man. His mother had taught him to worship idols, and he cared nothing for God.

When Ahaziah died, his mother saw her chance to become the ruler of Judah. She had all of his children killed so that none of them could become the new king or queen. Then she made herself the queen of the land! But one of Ahaziah's baby sons, Joash, was not killed. Some good people kept him hidden in the temple for six years. The high priest and his wife took care of him, and the queen didn't even know he was still alive. When Joash was seven years old, the high priest showed the little prince to the people who worked in the temple and said it was time to crown Joash as the real king of Judah. So they poured olive oil on Joash's head

and then put a crown
on him and shouted, "Long live the king!"

The wicked queen was arrested and taken
away. Then the high priest made a promise to
God that he and the young king, and all the
people, too, would love and worship only God.

*What promise did the high priest make? How
old was Joash when he became king?*
2 KINGS 11; 2 CHRONICLES 22–23

Jonah Runs Away

There once was a huge city called Nineveh. The people there did many wicked things.

One day God spoke to a prophet named Jonah and said, "Jonah, I want you to go to Nineveh and tell the people I am going to punish them because of their sins."

But Jonah didn't want to go, so he ran away to Joppa, a city by the sea. There he got on a sailing ship and sailed away. Jonah was trying to get away from God. So God sent a great storm. Soon the ship was ready to sink! The sailors were very frightened, and they prayed to the different gods they believed in to save them. The sailors woke up Jonah, who was asleep, and told him to pray too. Then Jonah told them he was running away from the One God, the God who had made the sea, and this was God's way of stopping him.

"What should we do to stop the storm?" the men cried out.

"Throw me into the sea," Jonah told them.

So the sailors threw Jonah into the sea, and immediately the sea grew calm and still. The sailors were amazed when they saw this, and promised God they would always worship him.

God sent a huge fish to swallow Jonah. Jonah was inside the fish three days and three nights. There he prayed to God and said he was sorry for disobeying him. God heard Jonah's prayer and made the fish swim to shore and spit Jonah out!

Then Jonah went to Nineveh with God's message. He told the people God would destroy the city because of their sins. When the people heard

this, they prayed to God to forgive them. When God saw that they stopped being bad, he took away his punishment and didn't destroy the city.

Where did God tell Jonah to go? What did Jonah do instead? Then what happened to Jonah?

JONAH

Good King Josiah

For hundreds of years there were wicked kings in the land of Judah. They set up idols for the people to worship. Soon no one went to the temple to worship God anymore. Then eight-year-old Josiah became king. As Josiah grew up, he loved God and wanted to obey him. So he went throughout the land and knocked down all the idols. Then he told his people to repair the temple so they could worship God there. While they were fixing the temple, one of the priests found the book in which Moses had written down God's laws hundreds of years before. The wicked kings and people of Judah hadn't cared to hear God's laws, and so the book had been lost and forgotten. But now when King Josiah read God's laws for the first time, he learned about the punishments God said he would send on the people for not obeying. Josiah was very sad

because he and his
people had not obeyed God. Then the king read
the laws to all the people. He promised God that
they would obey God's laws with all their heart
and soul.

*What did King Josiah do to the idols? What did
one of the priests find in the temple? What did
Josiah promise?* 2 CHRONICLES 34

Jerusalem Is Burned

God's people in the northern kingdom of Israel and in the southern kingdom of Judah had disobeyed God's laws for many, many years. There had been some good kings who helped the people to obey, but there had been many wicked kings who let the people worship idols. God's prophets had warned the people that they must stop sinning. They reminded the people that God is holy and must punish sin, but the people didn't listen. So God had allowed the people of Israel to be captured by enemies and made their slaves. Now God would punish the people of Judah too because they worshiped idols.

So God sent King Nebuchadnezzar of Babylon and his army to attack the city of Jerusalem in Judah. They surrounded the city for a year and a half and kept everyone from going in or out.

Soon the people had no food left. Then the enemy army broke down the walls of the city and burned God's temple and the palace and all the homes. King Nebuchadnezzar captured the people and took them back to Babylon as slaves.

But God is a loving God as well as a holy God. He loved his people and had a special plan to save them. His prophets had told God's plan to those who would listen. Someday, the prophets had said, God would send his own Son, the *Messiah,* to be their Savior and to take away their sins if they believed in him.

Why did God punish his people? Who was going to come to take away their sins? 2 KINGS 24–25; ISAIAH 53; MICAH 5

The Fiery Furnace

When King Nebuchadnezzar destroyed Jerusalem, he made many of the people go with him as his slaves to Babylon. Among the captives were four young men whose names were Daniel, Shadrach, Meshach, and Abednego. These young men loved God and were careful to obey God's laws. God blessed them because they were obedient, and he made them very wise. Soon the king chose them to be his helpers.

One day the king made a huge statue of gold and set it up where everyone could see it. Then he commanded all of his people to bow down and worship his statue. If they didn't obey, they would be thrown into a fiery furnace. But Shadrach, Meshach, and Abednego refused to bow down and worship the king's statue. They would only worship God. This made King Nebuchadnezzar angry. He gave them a second chance to obey his command, but the three men said, "We won't do it! If you throw us into the furnace, our God is able to save us, and he will. But even if he doesn't, we will not bow to your gold statue."

The king was furious. He commanded that the furnace be heated seven times hotter than ever before. Then his soldiers threw the three men into the furnace. The furnace was so hot the soldiers were killed by the heat.

But then the king saw an amazing thing. The three men in the furnace did not burn up. Instead, they walked around inside the furnace. The king also saw a fourth person in the furnace. It was an angel God sent to protect the men.

"Come out!" the king called to the three men, and they did. They were not hurt at all. Then the king believed that their God really was God!

Did Shadrach, Meshach, and Abednego obey God or the king? Suppose someone tells you to do something God doesn't want you to do. What will you do? DANIEL 1–3

TheWriting on the Wall

The new king of Babylon worshiped idols like Nebuchadnezzar used to do. One day he had a huge party. He used the gold and silver cups from God's temple as party dishes. He and his guests drank wine from them and got very drunk. Suddenly a hand appeared, writing words on the wall. But no one, not even the king's wise men, could read the strange words. Then the king sent for wise Daniel. When Daniel came, God showed him the meaning of the words.

"O king," Daniel said, "the words say that because you have disobeyed God, your kingdom has ended. God will give it to your enemies."

And that is just what happened that very night. The king's enemies slipped into the city, killed the king, and took over his country.

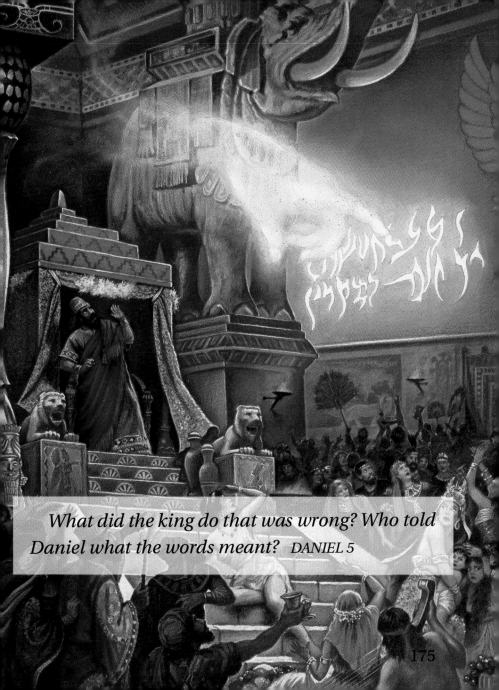

What did the king do that was wrong? Who told Daniel what the words meant? DANIEL 5

175

Daniel in the Lions' Den

The new king wanted to make Daniel a ruler over the whole land. But the king's other helpers were jealous of Daniel. So they tricked the king into making a law that would get Daniel in trouble. The law said that the people could not pray to God. They could only pray to the king! Of course, Daniel wouldn't stop praying to God. So the helpers punished Daniel for not obeying their law by putting him with hungry lions. But God sent an angel to shut the mouths of the lions so they couldn't hurt Daniel. When the king saw this, he told all the people in the land that Daniel's God was a powerful God and that his power would never end.

What did the king's helpers do to Daniel? How did God take care of him? DANIEL 6

176

Brave Queen Esther

One day the king picked a beautiful woman named Esther to become the queen. But the king didn't know that Esther was a Jew, one of God's people.

The king had a wicked helper named Haman. Haman hated a Jew named Mordecai because Mordecai would not bow down to him. So Haman decided to get even. He told the king that the Jews were bad; he told the king he should make a law that said all the Jews were to be killed on a certain day. The king believed Haman's lie and made this law.

Then Mordecai told Queen Esther to talk to the king. But it was very dangerous for anyone, even the queen, to bother the king if he hadn't sent for her. He might order that she be killed. But while all the Jews in the land prayed, brave Queen Esther went to the king. When the king saw her, he raised his gold scepter, which meant he wasn't angry. Then Queen Esther invited the king and Haman to a special dinner that night. The next night, she had another special dinner for them. There at the dinner, the queen begged the king not to let Haman kill her or her people, for she, too, was a Jew! Oh, how angry the king was at Haman! Because of his wickedness, Haman was hanged. Because of Esther's bravery, the Jews were not killed.

What did Queen Esther do that was brave? What happened to Haman? ESTHER

Jerusalem Is Rebuilt

The Jews were captives in the enemy land for many years before they were allowed to return to the city of Jerusalem. The city had been destroyed by King Nebuchadnezzar, so the people began to rebuild it. But even after many more years, the wall around the city still had not been rebuilt. Without a wall around it, the city was not safe. So a man named Nehemiah took charge and told all the other Jews to help him rebuild the wall. Some enemies decided to attack the workers and stop them from building the wall. So Nehemiah told the people to carry swords and spears while they worked. And so the walls around Jerusalem were rebuilt, and God's people had their special city once again.

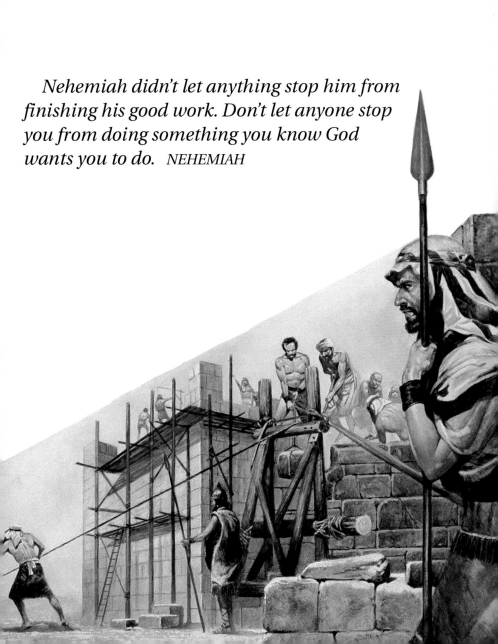

Nehemiah didn't let anything stop him from finishing his good work. Don't let anyone stop you from doing something you know God wants you to do. NEHEMIAH

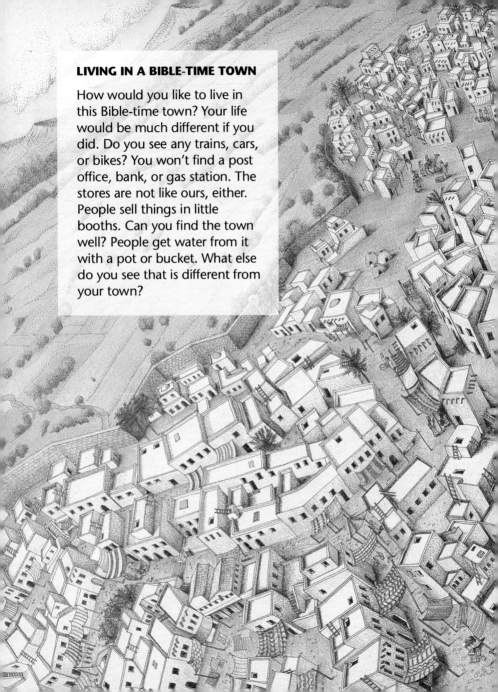

LIVING IN A BIBLE-TIME TOWN

How would you like to live in this Bible-time town? Your life would be much different if you did. Do you see any trains, cars, or bikes? You won't find a post office, bank, or gas station. The stores are not like ours, either. People sell things in little booths. Can you find the town well? People get water from it with a pot or bucket. What else do you see that is different from your town?

God's Special Messenger

Now the time came for Jesus, the Messiah, to come to earth to take away the people's sin, just as God had promised many years before. And how the world needed him, for everyone was selfish and unhappy. All the people in the world were sinners, just as Adam and Eve had been.

One day, the angel Gabriel came to visit a young girl named Mary. She was frightened when she saw him. But Gabriel said, "Don't be afraid, Mary. God has greatly blessed you. You are going to have a baby, and his name will be Jesus. He will have no human father, for he will be the Son of God."

Mary didn't understand how she could have a baby, for she wasn't married and was still a virgin. But the angel told her God would do a

special miracle to make her pregnant. How excited and happy Mary was at this wonderful news. She would be the mother of the Savior of the world!

What did the angel tell Mary? Who is Jesus' father? LUKE 1

Jesus Is Born

At this time the man who ruled the Jews told everyone to go back to the town where their relatives had lived hundreds of years before. So Mary and the man she was engaged to marry, whose name was Joseph, had to travel to the town of Bethlehem.

But when they got to Bethlehem, there wasn't any room for them at the little hotel in town, so they stayed in a stable where donkeys and sheep were kept. And while they were resting there, Mary's baby was born. Mary wrapped him in a blanket and laid him in a manger. And they named him Jesus, just as the angel had told them to.

Why did Mary and Joseph stay in a stable? Why did they name the baby Jesus? LUKE 2

Angels Appear to Shepherds

There were some shepherds in the fields outside Bethlehem watching their sheep to protect them from wild animals. Suddenly an angel surrounded by a bright light appeared to them. They were very frightened. But the angel said, "Don't be afraid; for I have good news for you and for all the world! Tonight, in Bethlehem, a Savior was born. His name is Christ the Lord!"

Suddenly many, many other angels appeared, praising God and saying, "Glory to God!

Peace on earth between God and man!"

After the angels returned to heaven, the shepherds said to each other, "Let's hurry to Bethlehem and find the baby!" So they ran to the village and soon found Mary and Joseph, and the baby lying in a manger. Afterwards, the shepherds returned to their sheep again, praising God for what the angel had told them. They told everyone they met that they had seen the Savior!

When the baby was eight days old, his parents took him to the temple in Jerusalem. There they met a wonderful old man named Simeon who loved God very much. He had been waiting many years to see the Savior whom God had promised to send. When he saw baby Jesus, Simeon took him in his arms and said, "Now, Lord, your promise has come true. I have seen the Savior. Now I can die in peace."

The shepherds wanted to tell all their friends about Jesus. We should tell our friends about Jesus too. It's the best news they will ever hear. LUKE 2

The Wise Men Visit

One day some wise men who studied the stars came to Jerusalem from a faraway land. They asked the king, "Where is the baby who will become the king of the Jews? We have seen his star in the sky and we have come to worship him."

The king was worried when he heard this. He was the king, and he didn't want anyone else to have his job. The king called in some priests and asked them if the Bible said where the new king would be born.

"Yes," they replied. "The prophets said he would be born in the town of Bethlehem." So the king told the wise men to find the baby in Bethlehem and then come and tell him so he could worship the baby too. But what he really wanted to do was to kill Jesus.

When the wise men found Jesus in Bethlehem, they worshiped him and gave him presents of gold and spices. But then God told them in a dream not to tell the king where Jesus was, so they did not go back to Jerusalem, but went home by a different road.

When the king found out that the wise men had disobeyed him, he sent his soldiers to Bethlehem to kill all the babies. But an angel of the Lord warned Joseph to escape to Egypt with Mary and baby Jesus. They stayed there for many years until the king was dead. Then they went to live in the city of Nazareth.

What presents did the wise men bring to Jesus?
What terrible thing did the king plan to do?
MATTHEW 2

Jesus Grows Up

Joseph and Mary went to Jerusalem every year to celebrate the Passover. When Jesus was twelve years old, he went with them.

After the celebration, they started walking back to their home in Nazareth, along with many of their friends and relatives. Joseph and Mary noticed that Jesus wasn't with them, but they thought he was walking with some of their relatives, so they didn't worry. But after a while they realized that Jesus wasn't there at all, and they were very worried. They hurried back to Jerusalem. They finally found Jesus in the temple talking with the great teachers there, listening to them and asking them questions. The teachers were very surprised at how much Jesus knew about the Bible.

"Why have you worried us this way?" Mary and Joseph asked Jesus.

Jesus was surprised. "Didn't you know I would be here at my Father's house?" he said. Then Jesus went back with them to Nazareth. There he grew strong and wise. He learned how to help Joseph in the carpenter shop, and he studied and learned about God, his Father.

Where did Mary and Joseph find Jesus? Why were the teachers in the temple surprised? LUKE 2

John Baptizes Jesus

Jesus had a cousin named John who told all the people that God's Son, the Messiah, was coming. He told them they needed to get ready by turning away from their sins. Those who listened to John and confessed their sins were baptized in the Jordan River to show that they had changed.

One day when Jesus was a grown man, he came to the river to be baptized by John. But John didn't want to do it. *"I* need to be baptized by *you,"* he told Jesus. But Jesus insisted on being baptized because God wanted him to do this. So John baptized Jesus. Then the sky opened up and God's Spirit came down in the form of a dove and landed upon Jesus. Then God spoke from heaven and said about Jesus, "This is my beloved Son. I am very pleased with him."

What happened right after Jesus was baptized? What did God say about Jesus?
MATTHEW 3

Jesus Is Tempted

After Jesus was baptized, he went into the wilderness for forty days and nights. There Satan tempted him to disobey God. Jesus didn't eat anything at all during that time. At the end of the forty days, he was very hungry.

Do you remember how Satan tempted Adam and Eve to disobey God? And when they did, it caused all the rest of us to have sinful hearts? Well, when Satan saw that Jesus had come to give us new, pure hearts and to make us good, Satan tried to stop him.

Satan said, "If you are the Son of God, change these stones lying on the ground into loaves of bread so that you will have food to eat."

But even though he was so hungry, Jesus told Satan that the Bible says it is more important to obey God than to have food to eat.

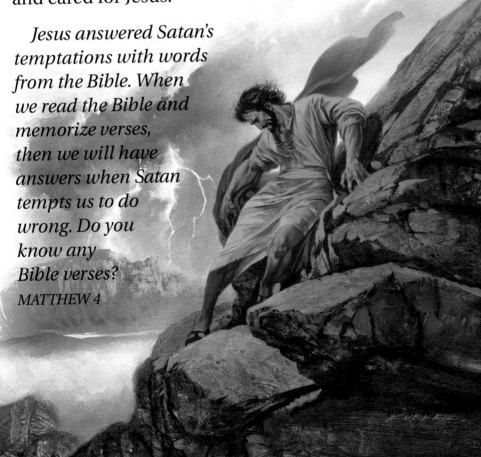

Satan tempted Jesus two more times—he even tried to get Jesus to worship him. But Jesus said, "Get out of here, Satan. It is written in the Bible, 'You shall worship only God and serve him alone.'" Then Satan left him, and angels came and cared for Jesus.

Jesus answered Satan's temptations with words from the Bible. When we read the Bible and memorize verses, then we will have answers when Satan tempts us to do wrong. Do you know any Bible verses?
MATTHEW 4

Jesus and His Disciples

After Jesus left the wilderness, many men and women came to listen to him. They wanted to learn from him. A few, like Peter, James, and John, became Jesus' special disciples and were with him all the time. They had to leave everything they had to become his disciples.

Later Jesus and some of his disciples went to the home of Peter and Andrew. Peter's mother-in-law was there, and she was very sick. Everyone begged Jesus to heal her. So he went in and held her hand and commanded the sickness to leave. Instantly she was well, and she got up and cooked dinner for them!

By evening a great crowd had gathered outside the house, bringing many sick people to be healed. And Jesus healed them all.

Peter and John and ten other men were Jesus' special disciples. Do you want to be his special disciple too? You can be, if you learn about Jesus and obey what he teaches in the Bible. MARK 1–2

Water Becomes Wine

Jesus, his mother, and his disciples went to a wedding in the city of Cana. When the family having the wedding feast ran out of wine to give the guests, Mary asked Jesus to help. So Jesus told the servants to fill up some big stone water jugs with water, right up to the brim. Then he said, "Take some to the man in charge of the feast." The servants did, and when the man in charge tasted it, the water had become the best-tasting wine! When Jesus' disciples saw this miracle, they believed that he was the Son of God.

What miracle did Jesus do? What happened when the disciples saw this miracle? JOHN 2

Jesus Clears the Temple

Jesus went to Jerusalem for the Passover celebration. While he was there he went to the temple and saw that it was being used as a market to sell cows, sheep, and doves to people who wanted to make sacrifices. Jesus was angry to find that the holy temple of God had become a store, so he made a whip of small cords and drove out all the animals and the men selling things. He also turned over their tables and poured out their money on the ground.

"My Father's house is a place for prayer, not a place for buying and selling!" he told them.

Why did Jesus chase away the people who were buying and selling things in the temple?
JOHN 2

Nicodemus Visits Jesus

One night a man named Nicodemus came to talk to Jesus. He told Jesus, "I know God sent you, for no one could do the miracles you do unless God were with him."

Then Jesus told him, "Unless you are born again, you cannot be one of God's children."

Nicodemus didn't understand. He thought Jesus was saying that he had to enter his mother's body again as a baby to be "born again." But Jesus explained that being *born again* meant asking God to give him new life—a life that would last forever. God loved the world so much that he sent Jesus to earth to die on a cross for all the sins of the world. Those who believe in him are forgiven and live forever!

What does born again *mean? Why did God send Jesus to earth?* JOHN 3

The Woman at the Well

One day Jesus and his disciples had been walking all morning in the hot sun. At noon they came to the town of Sychar. Just outside the town was a well where people came to get water. Jesus rested by the well while his disciples went into town to buy some food.

A woman came from the town to get some water. This woman didn't love God and had done many wrong things. Jesus knew this, for he sees each heart and knows everything we do. He talked to this woman and told her some of the bad things she had done. He also told her that God could give her a new life.

"Are you a prophet?" the woman asked.

"I am the Messiah," Jesus answered.

The woman ran back to the village and told everyone that she had met the Messiah. Then the

people invited Jesus to
stay for a while and
teach them.

*What did Jesus tell
the woman at the
well? What did she
do after she heard
this good news?*
JOHN 4

Catching Fish with Jesus

One day Jesus was preaching beside the Sea of Galilee. Because the beach was so crowded, Jesus got into Peter and Andrew's boat and taught the people from there. After he had finished teaching, Jesus told Peter and Andrew, "Go out into the lake and let down your nets, and you will catch a lot of fish!" Peter told Jesus they had fished all night and hadn't caught anything at all. But they obeyed Jesus anyway. They let down their nets and caught so many fish that the nets began to tear. They filled up two boats so full of fish that the boats almost sank!

What did Jesus tell Peter and Andrew to do? What happened? LUKE 5

A Hole in the Roof

Jesus was preaching to people who were crowded inside a house. Four men brought their sick friend on a stretcher so that Jesus could heal him. But it was so crowded they couldn't get in. So they went up on the flat roof, made a hole, and lowered the man down right in front of Jesus.

When Jesus saw that they believed in him, he said to the sick man, "Your sins are forgiven." Some of the religious leaders were angry when Jesus said this. They knew only God could forgive sins, and they didn't believe Jesus was God. Jesus knew what they were thinking. So, to show that he was God's Son and could forgive sins, he said to the man, "Get up and go home!" Then the sick man got up, picked up his stretcher, and went home! He was healed!

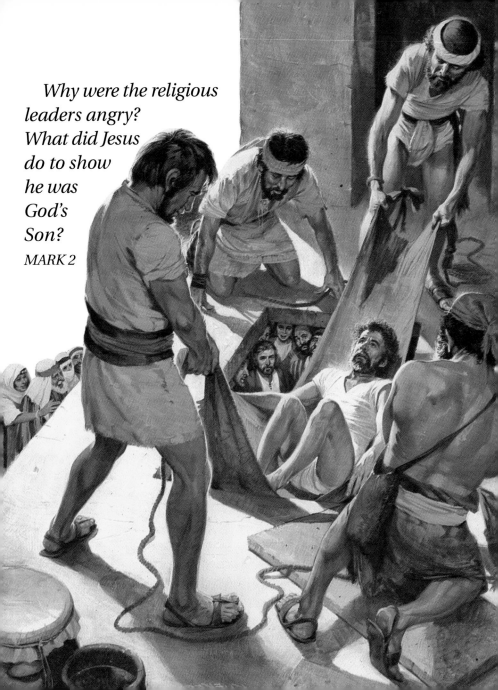

Why were the religious leaders angry? What did Jesus do to show he was God's Son?
MARK 2

Jesus Heals a Lame Man

Jesus went to Jerusalem to celebrate one of the Jewish holidays. On his way he passed a special pool of water. All around the pool lay sick, blind, and lame people. They were waiting there because every once in a while the water moved as if someone had touched it. The first person who got into the water after that was healed. Jesus saw a man there who hadn't been able to walk for thirty-eight years. Jesus felt very sorry for the crippled man.

"Do you want to be healed?" Jesus asked him.

"Of course!" the man replied. "But I have no one to help me into the water after it moves. Someone always gets there first."

Then Jesus told him, "Pick up your sleeping mat and start walking." And immediately the man was well!

When the religious leaders heard about this, they were angry. Jesus had healed the man on the Sabbath day, when no one was allowed to work. They did not care that Jesus was doing good things for people. From then on, they kept trying to get Jesus arrested.

How long had the man been crippled? How long did it take Jesus to heal him? JOHN 5

A Boy Comes Back to Life

Jesus climbed a hill and sat there with his disciples and taught the people who came to him. He told them that they should be humble, not proud, and that they should want to do right and please God. He told them they would be blessed if they didn't fight and tried to keep others from fighting. And he told them to be kind to everyone, even those who were unkind to them.

One day Jesus saw a funeral. A boy had died. How sad the mother was! Her husband had died before, and now her only son was dead too. So Jesus went over to the dead boy and said, "Young man, get up!" And the boy sat up, alive!

What did Jesus tell the people? What amazing thing did Jesus do at the funeral? LUKE 6–7

Jesus Stops a Storm

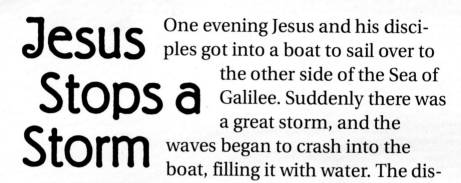

One evening Jesus and his disciples got into a boat to sail over to the other side of the Sea of Galilee. Suddenly there was a great storm, and the waves began to crash into the boat, filling it with water. The disciples were afraid. But Jesus was asleep.

"Master!" they shouted. "Save us. We'll all be drowned!"

Then Jesus stood up and spoke to the wind and the sea and said, "Peace! Be still!"

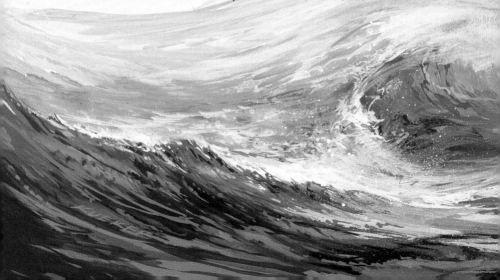

And the wind stopped blowing and the sea
became calm and still. The disciples were
amazed. Then Jesus asked them, "Why were you
afraid? Don't you trust me?"

*What happened when Jesus spoke to the wind
and the sea?* MARK 4

A Wild Man Is Healed

When Jesus and the disciples got to the other side of the lake, they met a wild man there who had evil spirits living inside him. These spirits made him run around without clothes on and act crazy and hurt others. People had tied him up with chains, but he had broken them and was now living in a graveyard.

The man fell down at Jesus' feet and worshiped him. The evil spirits inside him were frightened. They knew Jesus was God's Son and could make them go away. They begged him to let them go into a herd of pigs nearby, and Jesus told them they could. Then the herd of pigs ran over a cliff into the sea and drowned. Now the man was normal again, and he began telling everyone about Jesus.

What was wrong with the man in the grave-yard? Why were the evil spirits afraid of Jesus?
MARK 5

Jesus Heals the Sick

A Jewish leader came to Jesus and knelt at his feet. He told Jesus, "My little daughter is very sick and is going to die. Please come and touch her so that she will get well."

So Jesus and his disciples went with him, followed by a great crowd of people. But before they got to the house, a messenger arrived and told the little girl's father, "Your child is dead. Jesus doesn't need to come now."

But Jesus told the father, "Have faith, and she will be healed." Jesus meant that he should trust that Jesus could do anything, even bring the little girl back to life.

When they got to the house, Jesus went inside with the father, mother, and three of his disciples. Then he took the dead girl by the hand and

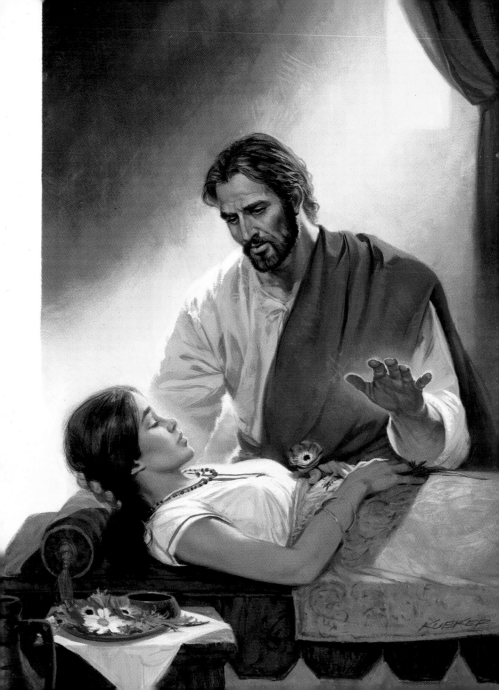

said, "Get up, little girl." And she jumped up and started walking!

Jesus continued healing the sick wherever he went, and large crowds followed him.

Why did the Jewish leader want Jesus to come to his house? What did Jesus do when he got there?
LUKE 8

The Miracle Picnic

Crowds of people followed Jesus out into the countryside. They wanted him to heal them and to teach them. So Jesus did. But as it grew late in the afternoon, the disciples got worried. "We don't have enough food for all these hungry people," they told Jesus. "Tell them to go home."

But Jesus said, "Don't send them away. Feed them."

Jesus told them to find out how much food they had. But no one had any food except a boy with a lunch of five very small loaves of bread and two small fish. Jesus told the disciples to tell all the people to sit down, for there were more than 5,000 people there that day. Then Jesus took the five small loaves of bread and two fish and thanked God for them. He broke the bread apart, and the disciples gave the bread to the people. There was enough for everyone to eat until all of them were full. There was even food left over!

How much food did Jesus start with? How many people did he feed? MARK 6; JOHN 6

Jesus Walks on Water

After the miracle picnic, Jesus told his disciples to get into their boat and cross to the other side of the lake. But Jesus went up into the hills to pray. Night came, and the disciples got caught in a storm out on the lake. Suddenly, they saw Jesus coming to them across the lake, and he was walking on the water! They thought he was a ghost. How scared they were!

"Don't be afraid," Jesus told them. Then Peter asked Jesus if he could walk to him on the water, and Jesus told him to come. Peter climbed out of the boat and walked on the water towards Jesus. But then he looked around at the waves and grew frightened. Suddenly, he started to sink! "Save me, Lord!" he cried, and Jesus reached out and saved him.

"Why didn't you trust me?" Jesus asked. Then

they climbed into the boat, and the storm
stopped.

*Why did Peter start to sink? When we stop trust-
ing Jesus, it's easy to get frightened.*

MATTHEW 14

A Good Neighbor

A teacher of the Jewish law asked Jesus what to do to have eternal life. Jesus asked him what the Jewish law said about this.

"Love God and your neighbors," he said.

"Yes," Jesus replied. "Do this and you will live."

"But who is my neighbor?" the teacher asked.

Jesus answered by telling him this story: A man was traveling from Jerusalem to Jericho, but some robbers stole his clothes and beat him up. They left him badly hurt by the side of the road. While he lay there, a Jewish priest came along. But instead of being kind to the hurt man, he crossed over to the other side of the road and went on, pretending he didn't see him. Next, a temple worker came along, but when he saw the hurt man, he also went by without trying to help him.

Then a Samaritan came by. (The Jews hated

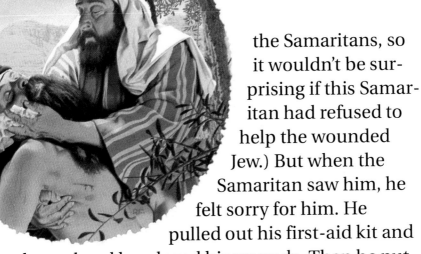

the Samaritans, so it wouldn't be surprising if this Samaritan had refused to help the wounded Jew.) But when the Samaritan saw him, he felt sorry for him. He pulled out his first-aid kit and cleaned and bandaged his wounds. Then he put the wounded man on his donkey, took him to a hospital, and paid the man's bill.

"Which of these three men was a neighbor to the hurt man?" Jesus asked.

"The one who helped him," the teacher replied.

Then Jesus told him, "Go and do the same." Jesus meant that people who say they love God must show it by being kind to others.

Is there someone you know who needs a friend? How can you be a good neighbor to that person? Do it right away. LUKE 10

233

Jesus Visits Mary and Martha

One day Jesus went to visit two sisters, Mary and Martha, and their brother, Lazarus. While Jesus was there, Mary sat at his feet to listen to him talking about the way to heaven. But Martha kept on working in the kitchen. She was angry with Mary for not helping her prepare dinner for their guest. She said to Jesus, "Don't you care that Mary has left all the work for me to do? Tell her to come and help me."

But Jesus said, "Martha, you get upset so easily. Only one thing is important, and Mary has chosen it." Mary had chosen to listen to Jesus, the very most important thing that any of us can ever do.

Do you spend time with Jesus each day by read-

ing the Bible and praying? Is anything you do more important than Jesus? LUKE 10

LIVING IN A BIBLE-TIME HOUSE

Can you find the things in this Bible-time house that are not the same as in your house? Where does the woman bake her bread? Can you find a TV or a place to take a bath? There is no electricity and no running water, and people bake bread outside in ovens heated by burning wood. What else can you find?

Jesus Defeats Death

One day, Jesus heard that Lazarus, Mary and Martha's brother, was very sick. When Jesus knew that Lazarus had died, he went to Mary and Martha's house. Martha ran out to meet him. "Jesus, if you had been here, my brother wouldn't have died," she said.

Jesus asked Lazarus's sisters and friends to take him to the tomb where Lazarus was buried. "Take away the stone from the front of the tomb," he told them.

Martha didn't want to do this, because the dead body would have already started to smell. But Jesus reminded her that they would see God's great power if they would trust him. So they moved the stone, and Jesus called, "Lazarus, come out!" And Lazarus came out! He had come back to life!

Many Jewish leaders believed in Jesus after see-

ing this, but others began planning to kill him.

God is the only one who can make dead people live again. This miracle shows us that Jesus is God.
JOHN 11

The Lost Sheep

Some Jewish leaders were angry at Jesus because he was kind to tax collectors, who cheated people whenever they could. Jesus knew what the leaders were thinking, so he told them this story: "If you have a hundred sheep and lose one of them, don't you leave all the others and hunt for the one that is lost? And when you find it, you take it on your shoulders and happily carry it home. Then you tell all your friends and neighbors that you have found your lost sheep, and they celebrate with you. Well, that's the way it is with these men who cheat. I have come to save them too, not just the good people." Jesus wanted sinners to come to him so he could teach them to ask for forgiveness and change their sinful ways.

God loves everyone. He wants everyone to know him as Savior. LUKE 15

The Runaway Son

Jesus told a story: "A father had two sons. The younger son demanded that his father give him his share of the family money. His father did, and the son left for a faraway country. He made lots of friends there, and spent his money on all sorts of bad things. When the money was all gone, his friends left him. So he got a job taking care of some pigs. He was so hungry that he wanted to eat the pigs' food.

"Finally he said to himself, 'Even my father's servants have more food than I do. I will go home and tell my father I have sinned against him and against God, and that I do not deserve to be his son. But I will ask if I can be his servant.' So he went home. His father saw him while he was still far off, and he ran to him and hugged him.

"Then the father said to the servants, 'Bring out my best suit of clothes and a pair of shoes for

him, and kill
the finest calf
and let's have
a party; for
this son of mine
was lost and is
found.' And what a party they had!"

Jesus told this story to remind the Jewish leaders that God loves sinners and is willing to forgive them.

What happened when the runaway son came home? God is like the father in this story, because he is always waiting to forgive us. LUKE 15

Jesus Blesses the Children

Jesus told a story about a proud Jewish leader and a cheating tax collector. Both of them came to the temple to pray. The Jewish leader thanked God that he was better than other people, especially the cheating tax collector. But the tax collector told God how bad he had been, and he asked for forgiveness. Then Jesus said a surprising thing. He said that the tax collector went home forgiven, and the proud man didn't! "Those who are proud will be brought low, but those who are humble and confess their sins will be honored," Jesus said.

One day some mothers brought their little children to Jesus so he could put his hands on them and bless them. Jesus' disciples wanted to send them away, but Jesus wouldn't let them. "Let the little children come to me," he said. "Don't tell them not to, for the kingdom of heaven belongs to them." He meant that only those who are humble and loving like little children will ever get into heaven. Then he took the children in his arms and blessed them.

Why was the tax collector forgiven, but not the Jewish leader? Why are children so special to Jesus?

LUKE 18

A Blind Man Is Healed

Jesus was on his way to Jerusalem, followed by crowds of people. A blind man named Bartimaeus was begging beside the road. He heard all the noise and asked what was going on.

"Jesus of Nazareth is coming," someone told him.

As soon as he heard this, Bartimaeus began to shout, "Jesus, son of David, have mercy on me!"

"Be quiet," everyone said.

But he just shouted louder, "Son of David, have mercy on me!"

Jesus stopped in the road and told Bartimaeus to come to him. So the blind man jumped up and went to Jesus.

"What do you want me to do for you?" Jesus asked him.

"Sir, I want to see," the blind man answered.

"All right," Jesus told him. "Because you have faith, you are well!" And immediately he could see! Then he followed Jesus down the road, praising God for the mighty miracle that had been done to him.

Do you want Jesus to do something special for you? Is it something God wants too? Then tell Jesus about it. MARK 10

Zacchaeus Climbs a Tree

Jesus was passing through a city where a tax collector named Zacchaeus lived.

Because he cheated people so much, Zacchaeus was very rich. As Jesus passed through the streets of the city, Zacchaeus tried to see him, but he couldn't because he was too short to see over the crowd. So he ran on ahead, climbed up into a sycamore tree, and waited for Jesus to pass by.

When Jesus came along, he stopped and looked up into the tree and saw Zacchaeus. "Come on down, Zacchaeus," Jesus told him. "I am going to your house for dinner." Happily, Zacchaeus climbed down. After he had been with Jesus, Zacchaeus became very sorry for cheating so many people. He promised to stop being unfair and to give half of his money to the

poor. Jesus
saw he was
sorry for his
sin, and he
forgave
him.

*Do
you
some-
times
do things
God
doesn't
want
you
to
do? What are they? Ask Jesus to forgive you, and
stop doing them.* LUKE 19

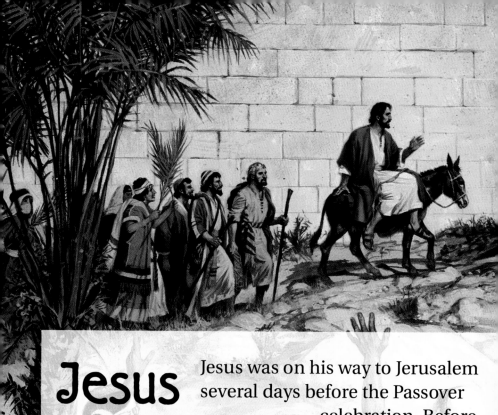

Jesus Rides into Jerusalem

Jesus was on his way to Jerusalem several days before the Passover celebration. Before he got there, he sent two of his disciples to a nearby village. "You'll find a young donkey there that has never been ridden," he told them. "Bring it to me. If anyone asks what you are doing, say 'The Lord needs him,' and they will let you have him."

The disciples found the young donkey just as Jesus said. As they were untying it, the owner asked what they were doing, and they answered, "The Lord needs him." Then the owner let them have the donkey. They brought it to Jesus and threw their coats on its back for Jesus to sit on.

As Jesus rode the donkey toward Jerusalem, a great crowd of people gathered. They spread their coats on the road in front of Jesus, while others cut down branches from the trees and made a green carpet for him to ride over. They did this to honor him, for this is what was done when a king rode through the streets. Then they began shouting, "Praise God for sending us a king!"

What did the people do and say as Jesus rode on the donkey to Jerusalem? MATTHEW 21; MARK 11

The Widow's Coins

One day a Jewish religious leader asked Jesus, "What is the greatest of God's commandments?"

Jesus answered, "You must deeply love the Lord your God. This is the first and greatest commandment. The next most important commandment is, you must love your

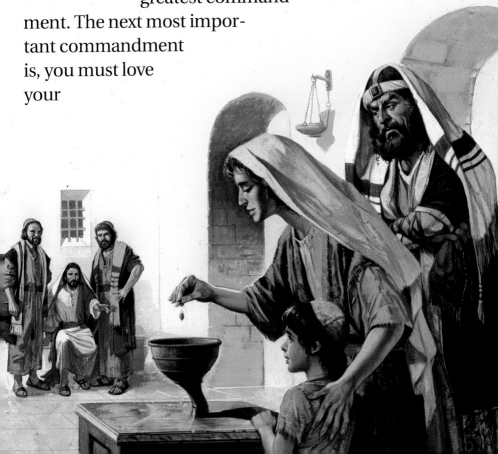

neighbor as yourself." Jesus said that all the other laws in the Bible are included in these two commands. If we obey these two greatest laws, we will be obeying all of God's other laws too.

Then Jesus went into the court of the temple, where the offering boxes were, and sat down and watched as people threw in the money they were giving to God. He noticed that many rich men gave lots of money, but a poor widow gave only two small coins! Then Jesus called his disciples and told them that the widow's small gift meant more to God than all the bags of money given by the rich men! For even though the rich men gave a lot, they kept most of their money for themselves. But the poor widow kept nothing—she had given the only money she had to God.

What are the two most important commandments? Why did the poor widow's gift mean more to God than the rich men's gifts? MATTHEW 22; MARK 12

Mary Shows Her Love

One day Jesus talked to his disciples about what would happen on the Judgment Day. He told them he will come back to earth in all his glory at that time. Everyone will stand before him. And he will separate those who have trusted in him from those who haven't. Jesus also told them that soon, at the Passover celebration, he would be betrayed and killed.

That night they ate supper at the home of Mary, Martha, and Lazarus. While they were there, Mary took a bottle of very rare, expensive perfume and poured it over Jesus' feet and

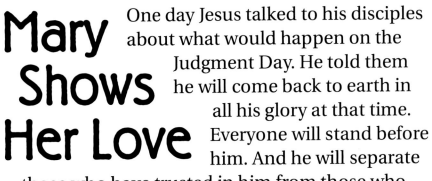

wiped them with her hair.

But Judas Iscariot, one of Jesus' disciples, complained about this. "Why wasn't this perfume sold and the money given to the poor?" he growled. But he really didn't care about the poor. He was a thief and wanted to steal the money if Mary had sold the perfume.

Jesus told Judas, "Leave her alone. She has done a good thing. You will always have the poor with you, and whenever you want to you can do them good, but you will not always have me."

Then Judas Iscariot went to the chief priests and told them that if they would pay him, he would help them capture Jesus.

Mary did a very special thing to show her love for Jesus. What did she do? What special thing can you do to show your love for Jesus? MATTHEW 25–26; MARK 14; JOHN 12

The Lord's Supper

Jesus and his disciples gathered in an upstairs room in Jerusalem to celebrate the Passover supper. The disciples started to argue about which one of them would be the greatest in God's new kingdom. But Jesus told them that those who wanted to be great must be humble servants to all. To show them what he meant, he got up from the table and began washing their dirty feet—a job a servant would usually do. Then Jesus told them that one of them was going to betray him. After this, Satan entered into Judas Iscariot. Judas left the table and went to betray Jesus to the chief priests, but the other disciples didn't understand what was going on.

Then Jesus picked up the bread they were going to eat. He blessed it, broke it apart, and gave it to his disciples. "This is my body," he said, "broken for you."

Then Jesus thanked God for the wine and gave it to them to drink. "This is my blood," he said. "It will be poured out for many." This was the first Holy Eucharist.

Then Jesus told them, "Do this in memory of me." His disciples followed his command and

met regularly for the "Breaking of the Bread,"
another name for the celebration of the Holy
Eucharist.

*What is another name for the "Breaking of the
Bread"?* LUKE 22; JOHN 13

Jesus Prays

After supper, Jesus and a few of his disciples went out to the Garden of Gethsemane. "Sit here while I go and pray," he told them. Then he went a little distance away and kneeled down and prayed. Jesus began to be in terrible distress and anguish as he thought about being punished for our sins and separated from his father, the holy God. Great drops of blood fell like sweat from his forehead to the ground. Jesus knew that in a few hours he would be crucified and die. But even though he didn't want to go through the agony, he told God that more than anything else, he wanted to do what God wanted.

When he got up from prayer and went back to his disciples, he found them sleeping. "Asleep?" he asked. "Get up and pray so that you will not be tempted to do wrong." Then he went away and prayed again. A second and even a third

time he came back and found them sleeping. Finally he told them, "Get up now, for my betrayer is near."

Judas Iscariot was coming into the garden with a gang of men sent by the Jewish leaders to capture Jesus. Jesus knew they were coming, but he didn't run. He knew this was God's time for him to die.

What was most important to Jesus, what he wanted or what God wanted? What is most important to you, what you want or what God wants?
MARK 14; LUKE 22

Jesus Is Arrested

Judas Iscariot had told soldiers and others with him, "The one I kiss on the cheek is the man you want." So Judas came up to Jesus in the garden, pretending to be his friend, and greeted him with a kiss on the cheek. This was the usual greeting between friends.

When his disciples saw what was going to happen, they shouted, "Lord, should we fight?" and Peter swung his sword and cut off the ear of one of the men arresting Jesus.

"Put your sword away," Jesus told him. "The angels could fight for me if I wanted them to, but that cannot be. I must die to save mankind." Then Jesus touched the wounded man's ear and healed it.

Then the soldiers grabbed Jesus and held him. Frightened now, the disciples ran away, and Judas and his men took Jesus to the high priest.

How did the soldiers know which one was Jesus? Why didn't Jesus fight or run away? MATTHEW 26; LUKE 22; JOHN 18

Peter Denies Jesus

When Jesus was arrested and led away, Peter followed far behind. Jesus was taken into the house where all the religious leaders were waiting. So Peter went into the courtyard and sat down among the servants beside a fire to keep warm.

A servant girl came over to him and said, "You were with Jesus!" But Peter said, "No, I wasn't!"

Another servant told some others, "This man was with Jesus of Nazareth." But again, Peter swore that wasn't true. "I don't even know the man!" he told them.

Later, a third servant asked Peter, "Didn't I see you in the garden with Jesus?" But Peter denied this too. Just then Peter heard a rooster crow, and he remembered something Jesus had told him. Jesus had said that before the rooster crowed, Peter would say three times that he didn't know

Jesus. When Peter realized he had just done this, he went away crying bitterly.

If we are afraid to tell others that we know Jesus, we are just like Peter. MATTHEW 26; LUKE 22

Pilate Judges Jesus

After they arrested him, the Jewish leaders asked Jesus, "Are you the Son of God? But when Jesus said yes, they spat on him and everyone shouted, "Kill him!" So they took him to Pontius Pilate, the Roman governor in charge of Jerusalem. But Pilate couldn't find Jesus guilty of any crime, so he sent Jesus to another Roman leader, Herod. Herod and his soldiers made fun of Jesus, but they couldn't find him guilty either, so they sent him back to Pilate. Pilate knew Jesus hadn't done anything wrong. But he didn't want the Jewish people to get angry at him, or he might lose his job. So Pilate handed Jesus over to be crucified. But first his soldiers whipped Jesus until he was bloody. Then they put a robe on him and a crown of thorns on his head and joked that he was a king.

Pilate knew what was right to do, but he didn't do it because he was afraid. Think about what you like best. Would you give it up if Jesus wanted you to? MATTHEW 26–27; LUKE 23

Jesus Is Killed

The soldiers made Jesus carry a heavy wooden cross up a hill outside the city. A crowd followed them out to Golgotha, where Jesus was to die.

Then the soldiers nailed Jesus' hands and feet to the cross and crucified him. Yet even though he was in so much pain, Jesus prayed that God would forgive the people hurting him.

Jesus hung there in agony for many hours, for crucifixion is a slow, painful death. The soldiers put a sign above Jesus' head that said, "Jesus of Nazareth, the King of the Jews."

Two thieves were crucified next to Jesus. One of them said angrily, "If you are God's Son, save yourself and us!" But the other thief said, "Lord, remember me when you come into your kingdom." To this thief Jesus said, "Today, you will be with me in paradise." Because the man believed in him, Jesus had forgiven his sins.

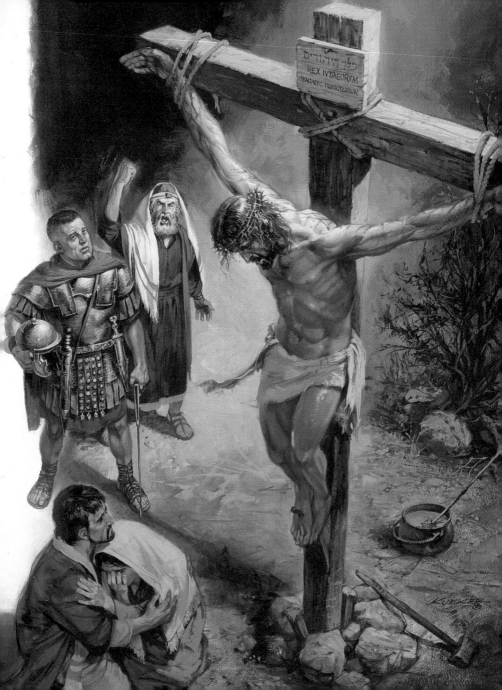

Then the sky grew dark. Finally, about three o'clock, Jesus called out, "My God, why have you left me?" He said this because our sins separated him from holy God. Then Jesus cried out, "It is finished," and he died.

That evening, one of Jesus' followers asked Pilate for Jesus' dead body so that he could bury it. When Pilate said yes, this man wrapped the body in a new cloth and laid it in a burial cave he owned. Then a huge stone was rolled across the opening. Pilate placed guards outside the tomb so that no one could steal the body and pretend that Jesus had come back to life.

What separated Jesus from God? Which thief would see Jesus in heaven? MATTHEW 27; LUKE 23

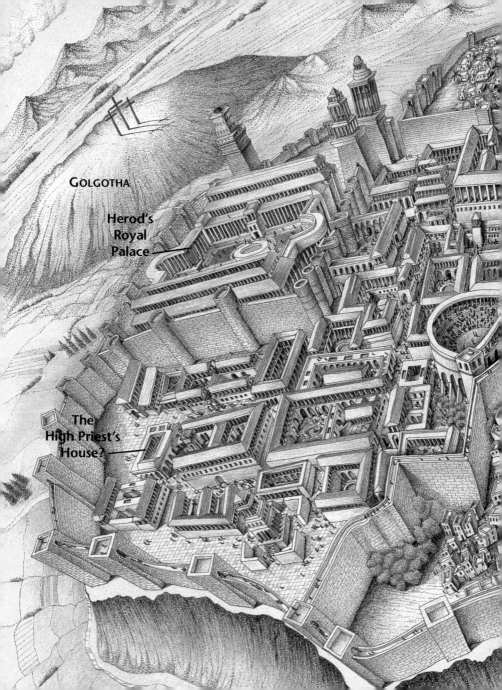

GOLGOTHA

Herod's
Royal
Palace

The
High Priest's
House?

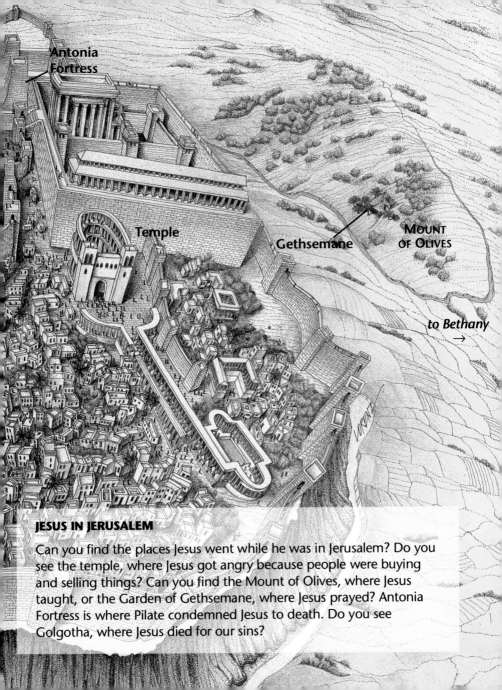

Antonia Fortress

Temple

Gethsemane

MOUNT OF OLIVES

to Bethany →

JESUS IN JERUSALEM

Can you find the places Jesus went while he was in Jerusalem? Do you see the temple, where Jesus got angry because people were buying and selling things? Can you find the Mount of Olives, where Jesus taught, or the Garden of Gethsemane, where Jesus prayed? Antonia Fortress is where Pilate condemned Jesus to death. Do you see Golgotha, where Jesus died for our sins?

Jesus Comes Alive Again

On the third day after Jesus died, the angel of the Lord came and rolled back the stone from Jesus' tomb. When the guards saw this happen, they fainted in terror. Early that morning, three women came to the tomb to put spices on Jesus' body. They were worried because they didn't know how they would move the heavy stone away from the tomb. But when they got there, the stone was pushed aside! They went into the tomb, and there was the angel.

How frightened they were! But the angel said, "Don't be afraid. Jesus isn't here; he has come back to life again. See, that is where he lay. Now go and tell his disciples that he is alive."

As the women were running to tell the disciples, Jesus met them, and they fell at his feet and

worshiped him. Then Jesus told them, "Tell my disciples I will meet them in Galilee."

Who rolled back the stone from the entrance to the tomb? Where was Jesus?
MATTHEW 28; MARK 16

Peter and John Visit the Tomb

When the women told the disciples what the angel said, Peter and John ran to the tomb to see for themselves. John got there first, stooped down, and looked in. He saw the cloth that Jesus' body had been wrapped in. Then Peter arrived and went right in and saw the empty tomb.

Finally they believed that Jesus had come back to life again. Before this, they hadn't understood what he meant when he had told them that he would be alive again the third day after he died.

Meanwhile, the frightened soldiers had told the religious leaders about the angel coming and rolling away the stone. The leaders paid the soldiers some money to lie and say the disciples had come and stolen the body. They did not

want anyone to believe that Jesus had risen from the dead.

What happened to Jesus' body? Did his disciples come and steal it? MATTHEW 28; JOHN 20

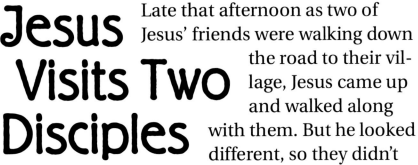

Jesus Visits Two Disciples

Late that afternoon as two of Jesus' friends were walking down the road to their village, Jesus came up and walked along with them. But he looked different, so they didn't recognize him.

When he asked them what they were talking about, they told him they had thought Jesus of Nazareth would free the Jews from the Romans, but instead, the religious leaders had killed him. They also told him that they had heard that morning from some friends that Jesus had risen from the dead. They were very confused. Then Jesus reminded them about what the prophets had written concerning the Messiah—that he would be killed, and that he would come back to life again.

When they got to their home, Jesus' friends invited him to spend the night there. As they were eating supper, Jesus took a loaf of bread, thanked God for it, and broke it apart. As he did this, suddenly they recognized him. Then Jesus disappeared!

The two quickly returned to Jerusalem. They found Jesus' disciples and told them how they had seen Jesus and talked with him, and how they had recognized him as he was breaking the bread.

Why didn't the two disciples recognize Jesus? What did he talk to them about? MARK 16; LUKE 24

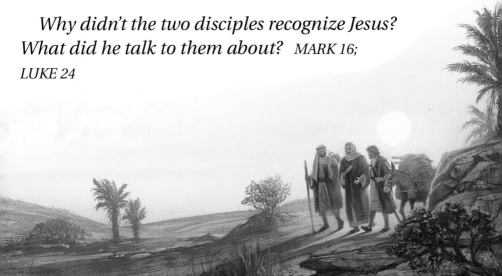

Doubting Thomas

The disciples were meeting together. Suddenly, Jesus appeared among them. They were very frightened, for they thought he was a ghost. But Jesus told them to touch him to see that he was real. Then he ate with them and explained to them what the Bible said about his death and coming back to life. Finally, the disciples understood.

One of the disciples, whose name was Thomas, wasn't there when Jesus appeared to them. When the disciples told him about it later, he didn't believe them. "Unless I see the wounds where he was nailed to the cross, I won't believe it was Jesus," he told them.

A week later, Thomas and the disciples were meeting together behind locked doors because they were afraid of the religious leaders. Suddenly, Jesus was standing there among them!

He said to Thomas, "Put your finger into my wounds, and believe!"

When Thomas heard his voice and realized it was Jesus, he said, "My Lord and my God!"

"Thomas," Jesus said to him, "you wouldn't believe until you saw me; but blessed are those who believe even though they haven't seen me."

Do you ever doubt that
God loves you or that he

will take care of you? He has said he will, so believe him. Don't be like doubting Thomas.

LUKE 24; JOHN 20

Jesus Returns to Heaven

Jesus appeared to his disciples several times. One of these times he told them, "Go and preach the Good News to the people of every nation, baptizing them in the name of the Father, the Son, and the Holy Spirit, and teaching them to do everything I have commanded you."

Forty days after he came back to life, Jesus appeared to the disciples in Jerusalem again. Then he walked with them to a place near the village of Bethany and blessed them. And while he was blessing them, he began to rise into the air until he disappeared into a cloud!

While the disciples stood there trying to see him, two angels appeared and said to them, "Why stand here looking at the sky? Jesus will return someday, just as you have seen him go!"

Where did Jesus tell his disciples to go and preach the Good News about his resurrection?

MATTHEW 28; ACTS 1

The Holy Spirit Comes

Then the disciples went back to Jerusalem to wait until God's Holy Spirit came upon them, for Jesus had told them to do this.

One day when they were meeting together, they heard what sounded like the roar of a great wind. Tongues of fire rested on the head of each of them, and the Holy Spirit came into them as Jesus had promised. Then they all began to speak in languages they had never known before!

There were many Jews in Jerusalem who had come from other countries to celebrate the Passover. These people were amazed to hear the disciples speaking in their own language. But others made fun of the disciples and said they were drunk.

Then Peter got up and preached. He was no longer the coward who had denied that he knew

Jesus. Jesus had forgiven him, and the Holy Spirit was with him, and now he wasn't afraid to speak about Jesus. He told the people that even though they had killed Jesus, God had brought him back to life. This proved that he was the Savior of the world whom the prophets had told about.

Many of the people believed Peter. How sorry they were that they had helped to kill Jesus. "What do we do now?" they asked.

Peter answered, "Turn from sin. Turn to God and be baptized, and the Holy Spirit will be given to you just as he was to us. For God has promised to send him to all who will obey him."

Thousands of people believed in the Lord Jesus that day and were baptized. They began meeting regularly together to learn more about Jesus from the apostles and to pray.

What happened to the disciples when the Holy Spirit came? What did Peter tell the people in Jerusalem? ACTS 2

Stephen Is Stoned to Death

The disciples, also called apostles, began to teach and preach about Jesus, and many people heard them and believed. The apostles even began doing miracles. The Jewish leaders did not like this and tried to stop them. They told the apostles they could not preach about Jesus, but the apostles wouldn't stop.

Stephen was a special man who loved Jesus. He preached about Jesus and did great miracles, and he helped the poor. To stop him, some Jews took him to court and made up lies about him. They told the high priest that Stephen said bad things about God's law. When the high priest asked Stephen about these things, Stephen told him and the judges how wicked they had been to kill Jesus. This made them furious. And when

Stephen looked up at heaven and said, "I see Jesus standing at God's right hand!" they dragged him outside the city and killed him by throwing stones at him.

But even while he was dying, Stephen prayed, "Lord Jesus, forgive them for this sin."

After Stephen's death, everyone turned against Jesus' friends and tried to hurt them.

What did the Jewish leaders tell the apostles to stop doing? Did the apostles obey? ACTS 6–8

Saul Meets Jesus

There was a religious leader in Jerusalem named Saul who began to hunt down and arrest the Christians. *Christian* is the name for those who believe that Jesus is the Messiah. Saul decided to travel to the city of Damascus to arrest the Christians there. As he was traveling, a bright light from heaven suddenly flashed down upon him. Saul was very frightened and fell to the ground. Then he heard a voice saying, "Saul, why are you trying to hurt me?"

"Who are you?" Saul asked.

The voice answered, "I am Jesus, the one you are hurting."

Then Saul believed in Jesus and was sorry for what he had done. Jesus told him to go on to Damascus. There God would show him what to do.

When Saul got up, he found that he couldn't see

anything. Those who were with him had to lead him to Damascus. There God gave Saul his sight again, and he met Christians and began preaching about Jesus. But the Jews there got angry at Saul and planned to kill him. Day and night, they watched at the city gates to capture him if he left. The Christians heard about this, so they helped Saul escape at night in a basket lowered from a window in the city wall.

What did Saul do to the Christians? What happened to Saul on the road to Damascus? ACTS 9

Peter Brings Dorcas Back to Life

The apostle Peter was traveling to different cities, preaching about Jesus and healing the sick. There was a woman named Dorcas in the city of Joppa who had always been kind and good and helped the poor. But she became sick and then died. So the Christians in the city sent for Peter. When he came they sadly showed him the room where she lay, and they showed him all the clothes she had made for the poor.

Then Peter asked everyone to leave. After they left, he kneeled down and prayed. Then he said to the dead body, "Dorcas, get up!"

And she woke up, as though she had been asleep, and sat up, and Peter gave her back to her friends!

Why was Dorcas so special? What miracle did Peter do? ACTS 9

Peter and the Angel

King Herod began to hunt the Christians and put them in jail and kill them because he saw that this pleased the Jewish leaders. He killed John's brother, James, and he also arrested Peter and planned to kill him too.

While Peter was in jail, the Christians in Jerusalem kept praying for him. The night before he was to be killed, an angel suddenly appeared in the jail. The chains holding Peter fell off, the jail doors opened, and Peter followed the angel outside.

Then Peter hurried to find the Christians who were praying for him, and knocked on their door. The girl who went to open it recognized Peter's voice and could hardly believe it was him! She left him standing outside the door and ran to tell the other Christians, but they wouldn't believe it

was Peter! Finally they let him in. How excited and happy they were that God had answered their prayers and saved Peter.

How did Peter get out of jail? What happened when he came to the house where the Christians were praying for him? ACTS 12

Paul and Silas in Jail

Saul, who was now called Paul, became a missionary and traveled to other countries, preaching about Jesus. He wanted everyone, not just Jews, to hear about Jesus and be saved from their sins.

A Christian named Silas was also traveling with Paul. In the city of Philippi, some people got angry at Paul and Silas for preaching and casting out evil spirits. So Paul and Silas were beaten and then thrown into prison. The jailer was told he would be killed if they escaped.

In the middle of the night, as Paul and Silas were praying and singing to God, there was an earthquake that shook the whole prison. All the prison doors flew open, and the chains on the prisoners fell off.

When the jailer saw that the doors were open, he thought all the prisoners had escaped, and he took out his sword to kill himself. But Paul called out, "Don't hurt yourself. We are all here."

The jailer saw that no one had tried to escape, and he came to Paul and Silas and asked what he had to do to be saved. So they told him about Jesus, and the jailer and his family became Christians.

In the morning, the city officials let Paul and Silas go.

What is a missionary?
What happened that
made the jailer want
to become a Chris-
tian?

ACTS 16

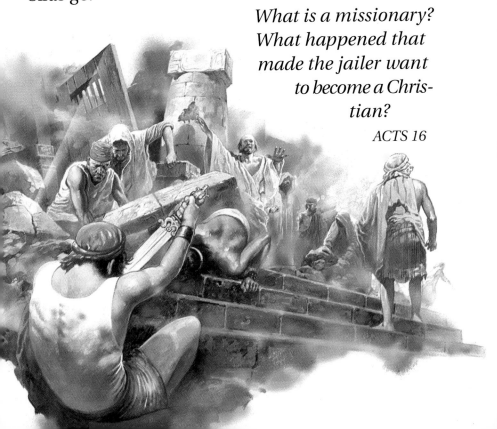

Shipwrecked!

Paul went to many cities and preached about Jesus, and many people became Christians. The Christians in each city got together and formed a church, and they met together regularly to read the Bible and to pray. Paul visited these churches and wrote letters to them. Some of these letters we now have in our Bible. They are called Epistles.

But the religious leaders hated Paul and wanted him arrested. When Paul finally went back to Jerusalem, they grabbed him and were about to kill him when a Roman army captain stopped them. The captain sent Paul as a prisoner to the Roman governor. The Roman governor and other officials heard Paul's story and realized that he had done nothing wrong. But the religious leaders insisted he must die. Finally,

Paul asked to be taken before Caesar in Rome. He wanted Caesar to judge his case.

So Paul was put on a ship and began the journey to Rome. When the ship stopped at the island of Crete, Paul warned the captain that if they went on, the ship might sink. But the captain wouldn't listen and sailed on. Soon there was a violent storm that lasted many days. Finally the ship began to sink. Paul told the frightened soldiers not to be afraid. An angel had told him no one would die.

And that is just what happened. The ship sank near an island, and everyone made it to shore alive. Then, as they were building a fire on the beach to keep warm, a poisonous snake bit Paul. But it did not hurt him, and the people watching were amazed.

When Paul got to Rome, he preached to the Jewish leaders there. These Jews were willing to listen to him and did not try to hurt him. Some of them even believed in Jesus.

What did the Christians in each city do? In what ways did God take care of Paul? ACTS 21–28

John's Vision

Jesus' disciple John was now an old man. The leaders of Rome had sent him to live on a lonely island so that he couldn't preach about Jesus anymore. But God had not left John. God showed him an amazing vision—a picture of wonderful things that God would do in the future. John wrote about this vision in a letter to some of the churches.

John's letter tells about what will happen when the world ends and what heaven will be like. It tells about Jesus coming back to earth to take all the

Christians home to heaven with him. How exciting it must have been for the persecuted Christians to hear that Jesus will come again, and that all those who believe in him will be a part of his kingdom. What good news it was to know that Satan and the sin that he causes will be crushed forever. This is exciting news for us too!

Jesus is now in heaven. Will he come back to earth again? REVELATION